Make it Happen! Discover the

SECRETS

to Success in Sales

Harold Antor

Make It Happen!: Discover the Secrets to Success in Sales focuses on the importance of maintaining a positive and resilient attitude in sales. It emphasizes that a "winning attitude" is not just about being optimistic or friendly but involves mental toughness, motivation, and a hunger for success. It points out that a game plan helps identify necessary resources and changes to achieve goals. The author shares a personal journey of realizing the need for further education to improve sales performance, illustrating how new skills and strategies can lead to significant professional growth.

It further advises setting daily targets and using a game plan to stay focused amidst distractions. It emphasizes tracking progress and adjusting plans to maintain momentum toward achieving goals. Then, it highlights the necessity of working efficiently and understanding that time is money in sales. The quicker a salesperson can close a deal; the sooner they can move on to the next opportunity.

The personal stories add authenticity and depth, encouraging readers to reflect on their planning processes and consider how they might apply these lessons to their personal and professional lives. It motivates a mindset of continuous improvement and warns against complacency. It suggests that even when performing well, one should always strive to do better.

Moreover, it advises salespeople to overcome fear, especially when dealing with high-profile clients. It shares a personal story of overcoming intimidation and learning that people are just people, regardless of their status.

Overall, the book provides practical advice and personal anecdotes to illustrate the mindset and behaviors necessary for success in sales. It emphasizes resilience, continuous improvement, and the ability to handle rejection and fear.

— *Reviewed by Book Critic Trisha Mowler*

978-1-965552-13-1 (Paperback)
978-1-965552-14-8 (Hardback)

Library of Congress Control Number: 2025905683

BOOKWRIGHTS
HOUSE

admin@bookwrightshouse.com
☎ (213) 286 6700

ACKNOWLEDGMENTS

Four years ago in 2017, writing a book was the last thing on my mind. The fact that I am here at this point is due in large part to the urging and encouragement I have received from my family members and friends who I wish to recognize all of them here some, by name and others in the general umbrella of those who have made a contribution.

I want to say thank you to my wife, Sabrina, who in 30 years of marriage has been a rock of encouragement and support. I say thank you to my three children Harold Devaughn, who has been and still is urging me along in this journey to share my life's experiences with others as an encouragement and not keep it a secret. The same goes for Shannon, my daughter, who has always believed in me and expressed her love and appreciation for me. My last child, Jonathan, who literally sat me down and impressed on me the value that my story of struggle and success can bring to so many if I would only share it more often and who tells me how proud he is of me when he sees me in forums and formats like my course sharing my knowledge and experiences with others. I thank my siblings, especially my big sister, Weldene, who, being in real estate is a continuous source of encouragement.

I thank my great business partner and friend Corinna Neely who takes the time from time to time to share encouraging and uplifting words to remind me of strides that I have made and that we have made together to overcome so many challenges to realize the achievements that we have made as a team. Also, I want to thank my lifelong friend, Mark Smith, and my team members who have supported me in this sales training endeavor by encouraging, attending, and sharing in my venture. These persons include Chantilly Miller, Carol Rahming, Delissa Dawkins, Fernella Gordon, Dominique Moss, Jennifer Richards, Tiphany Maycock, Terry Demeritte, and others.

This book started out as a seminar, then an online course, and now a book. I want to thank all of those people who attended my courses and bought my online course which gave me the impetus to write this book as I saw the need and interest in the subject matter from persons in many different fields of endeavor. They also gave me the reassurance that what I had to share was valuable to them and others.

Finally, I cannot forget, and I give a special shout out and thank you to the person who started it all, Mr. Deon Knowles, a former employee of mine who invited me to speak at a seminar he held for small business owners. It was from that seminar and the positive response I got that led to the seminars, the course, and this book. Thank you for the opportunity.

To all of those, I know I'm missing some names, who have made a contribution to this journey, thank you.

FOREWORD

If you are in sales or thinking about getting into sales, you should read this book. As an author myself and a sales coach, I have seen firsthand the impact great training and information can have on the success of a salesperson who applies successful knowledge and actions in their work. I have also seen the other side where far too many persons in this life-changing opportunity called sales have squandered their good fortune by having access to great information, training, and coaching but decide not to take advantage and inevitably wither in the field and fade away. There is an old saying that goes, "nothing happens in business until a sale is made". Sales are the goose that lays the golden egg and especially in those industries like insurance, real estate, and car sales, among others that depend on salespeople doing a good job, sales is critical. It is literally lifeblood. Companies are desperate for great salespersons who can deliver results on a consistent basis and make a great living for themselves in the process. It is no secret that a large percentage of people who enter the sales field fail in their first year or so and it is no secret that many persons in sales now are not performing at acceptable, much fewer outstanding levels. It really makes you stop and wonder why. What is the secret sauce, that magic potion or illusive spell that makes the difference? How is it that some people seem to find it and so many do not?

Well, that is why I am so excited that Harold has decided to write this book, Make It Happen. Harold has done an incredible job of taking the mystery out of success in sales and making access to the secrets to success available to all. He has laid it bare. Over the years, I have read many a good book on sales, each with its own bend. In this book, Harold holds your hand and walks you through the secrets to success like an experienced guide through a crowded maze. Along the way, he livens up the trail by sharing real experiences from his personal journey from a life of poverty and want to a place of comfort and a life full of accomplishment, love, and bright hope. As I read his actual experiences, I felt his emotions and his desire to succeed. More importantly, I found myself engrossed in each secret as he unveiled their value and how to implement each one in my own day to day experience. There is much to be learned or reminded here. I can see how this book can in fact help anyone reading it to Make It Happen in their life as well.

Harold has been in sales for over 30 years and it shows. His wealth of experience to draw from allows him to make his points clearly and give examples from his experience about how he has applied the concepts that he shares in this book. Make It Happen is a clarion call to all salespersons to pull the best out of themselves, to challenge their current status, and set a course to unchartered achievement levels in their career.

Eliot Kelly is a renowned speaker and sales coach. He is a bestselling author. His books include The Eye of the Needle: The Cost Of Success, Ahead of the Storm, Inside Out: It An Inside Job, and Creating A Platinum Lifestyle: Set Your Mind On Fire. In addition, he is a Radio and TV personality, a Podcaster, and an Entrepreneur. Mr. Kelly has a Master's Degree from The Manchester Metropolitan University and a Post Graduate Certificate in Academic Practice and Higher Education.

CONTENTS

CHAPTER 1

You can Predict Your Future by Creating it Today

What makes the difference between the high-flying successful salespersons and the average salespersons? What do they do that brings them so much success and consistent success? What are their secrets? We all look at those highflyers with admiration, in awe and sometimes in confusion because we just cannot figure it out. These people are often revered, sometimes envied, but always respected. I know I admired them, respected them and wanted to be like him. Successful salespeople live so well. They drive nice cars, often live in large fancy homes, they dress well, and their children go to private schools, they walk around with an "Air" about them, they exude confidence, not arrogance, confidence, and you know what, they should. They have earned that confidence because they have figured it out. They have figured out the secrets to success in sales.

The purpose of this book is to help you become one of them, and if you are already one of those highflyers, first of all, welcome and congratulations, second, let's talk about how you can move your game to an even higher level.

There is a lingering question here, and that question is this, what constitutes a highflyer, successful salesperson? And more to the point, how can I become one? I'm happy you asked. The fact of the matter is that a review of different settings and industries may yield a different answer to that question, particularly if the determinant is number of units sold or dollar volume of sales or total commissions earned. I would consider an above average performance in any of these metrics a fair means of measuring success.

However, you do not have to search too far to find out a few points of concern that prevail in the world of sales. First, and quite unfortunately, many people fail at their first foray into sales. In May 2017, Inc. magazine ran an article by Tim Askela under the caption "Why Sales Hires Fail 75% percent of the Time—within the First Year," with a subheading, "Money does not incentivize sales." That is a staggering figure, 75%…within the first year! Sure, there are a number of reasons for that, but it's fair to say that if more of those persons experienced sales success early and more consistently, more of them would have stuck around. As a support to Inc.'s article and to show how longstanding and pervasive this problem is, let me draw your attention to a report by Rathbone Results, a UK-based consultancy firm that was published on ISM (Institute of Sales Management), online page. The report decries the observation "that on average 51% of the sales force population are failing to achieve their targets." Now, one might say that even though that is not good news, but so long as the company and salespersons are making money, that may not be such a bad problem. Well, the report goes on to say, quote, "The average cost of a salesperson within the UK is circa L60,000 per annum, and that in contrast to the average UK salary which according to the High Pay Centre research (2016) is L28,200." End quote (about US 38,000).

The report cites as a problem, "Recent studies have indicated that the top twenty percent of the sales force produce sixty two percent of the revenue (sales). Things are not that much different in the US. In an article published on LinkedIn in 2019, Kathleen Roberge, Chief Revenue Officer at Landit writes, "why do only 67% of sales reps hit their quotas (For Entrepreneurs and The Bridge Group) and why are 80% of sales closed by only 20% of the salespeople (linked In)? If you research salespeople driven industries like insurance, Real Estate, Car sales, and salespeople generally, you find that income ranges are on average around $40,000.00 give or take. Now listen, I am not one to be ungrateful or to diminish people's accomplishments. In a world where many people find it difficult to find food, $40,000.00 is a good income. This book is not about that. I have been fortunate to find myself in a sales career because in this career you can achieve levels of income through your own willingness to prepare yourself and hard work that often cannot be found in the usual corporate environment. A sales career is really an opportunity to change your life by substantially improving your income. If you are in sales or considering sales, this book is designed to show you how to move your income upwards 25%, 50% 100% or more. Imagine that. What would you do with a sustained increase of any one of those percentages to your income? My message to you is that if you apply the information in this book, you will be able to achieve that and more. You will become one of those highflyers, you will be admired and awed. You will achieve your dreams. In this book I will share with you how to organize your mind and your actions to be successful. I will share with you proven sales strategies that I've used, closing approaches and techniques that work, you will learn what to say in sales engagements, how to identify markets and most importantly, how to light a fire under yourself to keep your motivation strong. I want you to be excited about your sales job because you, too, figured out how to apply the secrets to success. Let me share a bit of my story with you, so you can see why I am so passionate about the sales opportunity, how it changed my life and how it can change yours.

In June, 1998, I qualified to attend the Million Dollar Round Table (MDRT) Annual Meeting in Chicago. This was my second qualifying year and my second round table meeting. My first was the previous year in Atlanta, Georgia. That was a great meeting, eye opening, and it filled me up for the next year. Now, I was here, all smiles, so proud of myself. Why? Because I actually belonged. I was a bonified member of The Million Dollar Round Table, "The Premier Association of Financial Professionals", that's their actual tagline, and I was one of them. The Million Dollar Round Table is an Association of the top 1% of life insurance financial advisors, or salespersons, worldwide. Simply put, I was among the best and one of the best in the world. The membership of MDRT is made up of insurance professionals from eighty two (82) countries. There are more than 39,000 members.

I came from a life where usually when there was a special meeting going on, where "important" people were attending an event, you know, VIPs, I would either be the guy serving at the event or the guy being rejected at the door because he did not belong. "This is not for you." So at these meetings, I felt an extra thrill to walk up to the door, show my badge, and enter.

The meetings were held at the Hyatt Regency Chicago. I stayed at the Sheraton Grand Chicago just across the river. Beautiful, just beautiful. I'd walk right across the bridge to attend the meetings. The meetings are arranged where every morning at 8am everyone gathers in a huge auditorium for the main platform presentations. There, high level speakers would address the gathering of 8 – 10,000 members from literally all over the world. After the main platform we break out into smaller meetings called Focus Sessions. One Focus Session in particular, changed my life.

I saw the name on the program, but I thought it was a misprint because it could not be true. I had to attend to see what was up. The session was called "You can predict the future by creating it today." Yep, I can hear you now. You're thinking exactly what I was thinking, no way. So, I thought, this I had to hear. I really cannot remember the name of the speaker, but the room was packed with members and the anticipation was great and thick. So it seemed, many people were thinking the exact thing I was thinking. Then he appeared. With a big smile and a confident air about him, he began to make his case. All Focus Session speakers are MDRT members so he was one of us and knew our business. I listened very attentively, at first with some apprehension, then he started to make some sense. He was not selling mumbo jumbo or abra kadabra. His point was simply this; no, you actually cannot predict exactly what is going to happen in the future nor do you have magical powers to make the future how you want it, but in a sense you do. This is where I leaned in. He said if you learn your business, understand your client's needs, work hard using the production guidelines that are shared at MDRT, if you are honest and caring about your clients, well, you can predict the future. You will have a great business, make a very good, if not exceptional income, have great relationships with your clients and your colleagues, and, well, you would have created your future. That way of seeing things blew me away. I felt, wow, there is a path, you can actually build a better future, and yes, I do have a say in how my life turns out. To this day I still reflect on that, "You can predict the future by creating it today" idea. If there is one message I would like to leave with you it is this, your life, your future is not in the hands of someone out there. Listen, trust me, I know that there are things, situations, and people out there who and what you cannot control, but if you do those things, regardless of what business you are in, if you learn your business, understand your clients' needs, work hard, if you are honest and caring with people, you too, can predict and create the future you want for yourself.

I guess for me his message was especially impactful because for the first time somebody was giving me hope that I can have a better life than I had experienced in my past. Even though I was in my early thirties, married with two young children, and even though I had qualified for MDRT for two consecutive years, I was working very hard and consistently just to not lose my place, to not fall back to where my life was, but this time with my own wife and children in the misery with me. I was afraid of that. His message helped to calm me down by assuring me that, all things being equal, follow this process and you will be ok. That is my message to you in this book.

Just a little about me so you have an appreciation of where I came from. I was born to immigrant parents on Grand Bahama, one of the islands of the Bahamas. The Bahamas is the most beautiful country in the world and I love living here. However, in America, when people say they come from immigrant parents, that is often a badge of honor and welcomed. In the Bahamas, that is not necessarily so, certainly not for people like my mother who came to the Bahamas from Haiti on a boat in the 60s and entered illegally. Most Haitians in the Bahamas come illegally, even today, and live in sub-par conditions throughout their lives in the Bahamas. My situation was no different. Mine was a single parent household with six children for my mother to care for. I am the oldest son. My mother has little formal education and held low paying, menial domestic jobs. There was no father around, in fact, I met my father twice in my life for about an hour each time. I have not seen him for a least thirty years. My children have never seen him. As you might imagine, growing up we experienced some very difficult times. By the time I was 13 years old, we had moved at least eight times. We were kicked out several times and forced to live in some God-forsaken places. One place was a condemned apartment that my mother had to beg the owner to allow us to stay in. No one had lived in that building for years. When we moved in, there were no kitchen cabinets, nor running water, an open cesspit in front of the yard that was covered by plywood, every window in the apartment was broken, there were no tiles or carpet on the floors, only hard, cold concrete and the studs for carpet all around the edges of the floor. There was no door knob on the front door. We had to tie it closed every night with a string. That was one place. We eventually moved from there into a one bedroom apartment in the ghetto where all six of us slept in one room and shared one bathroom. At that place, we lived around drug dealers and from time to time I would watch them sell cocaine and marijuana, and, believe it or not, I would watch police officers drive up in the police car to buy their drugs. In that world, you grow up very fast. Innocence was a fantasy. From there we moved to another God-forsaken place with no running water, no kitchen cabinets, the cesspit backing up into the shower and still sharing one bathroom. This place was so bad, the Landlord stopped collecting rent.

While all of this was going on, to help make ends meet, I, as the oldest son, had to get a full time job as a Busboy from 14 years old. Every day after school I would rush home, change into my busboy uniform and head out to the hotel for my 4pm – 12pm shift. After work, I would get home, do my homework and get to bed between 2am – 3am and got up 7am for school. Every morning, I would share my tips from the night before with my siblings for their lunch money. This went on for years. Actually my mother and I worked at the same hotel. She got the job for me. She was a Dishwasher and I was a Busboy. I would bring in the dirty dishes in from the dining room to her. I never saw my pay check because they would give it to her for me and she would do what she had to do. Sometimes we would go weeks without seeing each other because when she worked the 7am – 3pm shift, she would be getting off and heading home when I was coming from school, rushing home to get to work for 4pm.

I eventually quit that job. It was getting too much. I graduated high school, with honors, and set out to find a job, still living at home and in the same God-forsaken place. I finally found a job at a bank, by that time the hotel where my mother worked had closed down. I was the only breadwinner in the house. This situation lasted for a few years. There were many times when I began to lose hope. I thought that my life was relegated to this state of being and I grew more frustrated every day. If it were not for my faith in Christ and my church family, I am sure I would have lost my mind.

When I was seventeen, just out of high school, a friend introduced me to the Amway business. Through Amway, I learned about dream building and setting goals and more importantly, writing down your goals. So I did that. One night in 1987, I sat down in that same apartment and wrote down my dreams. Clearly influenced by the big beautiful homes I saw when I drove around, and the flashy cars, the first thing I added to my list was I wanted a big, beautiful spilt level house. I didn't even know what that meant, but it sounded good as I heard other people talk about it, I wrote down the kind of cars I wanted, where I wanted to live, what I wanted to do for my church, my family and in ministry. I wrote all those things down. I still remember doing that and how good it felt just to be in that space mentally. I folded that piece of paper up and put it in my wallet. I carried that around with me for about seventeen years. I will share the story about how I lost that paper later on in the book, which in itself was a mind blowing experience.

Obviously there is much more to this story, but I wanted to give you enough so that you would appreciate why the message that you can predict your future by creating it resonated with me so much. His words gave me hope that I can have a hand in making sure that my past life stayed in the past and my future can be as bright as I was prepared to make it through learning and hard work. At the time that I attended that session in 1998, that piece of paper was right there with me in my wallet in Chicago. I had not yet achieved many of the dreams that were written on it. But as I write this book, I am so happy and so proud to say that not only have I achieved the things I wrote on that piece of paper, I have gone so much further. In that document, I did not contemplate having my own children and providing a better life for them despite my background. I am therefore again happy to report that I have three wonderful children, all of whom have gone to great schools and colleges and all with one wonderful wife with whom I've been married for 30 years. You can predict your future by creating it today.

There is a notion that when you set a goal and you are serious about it by making moves to achieve it, that the cosmos, the stars, fate, the power of God, begin to work in your favor, sometimes unbeknownst to you, to bring your goal to fruition. My life experiences have lead me to believe that that is true. As I indicated, I sat down in 1987 and wrote out my dreams/goals on that paper for 1987 – 1997. At that time, I was working at the bank as a teller and it was clear to me for a number of reasons that my future was not there, but I could not leave. One night after church, a friend of mine who was in the insurance sales business approached me and out of the blue said to me, "you know Harold, you would do good in the insurance business." What he meant was insurance sales. Even though I had done some sales before, if you can call them sales; I sold newspapers, I shined shoes, sold Encyclopedias, sold alarm systems, Amway products, conch shells, straw dolls and baskets and necklaces to tourists, etc., I did not consider those activities a "sales job." He was propositioning me to leave my "good job" at the bank and go into "selling" insurance. It in fact could have been real estate, computers, or anything else. He just happened to be in insurance sales. Even though I was broke at the time—this was in 1988, within a year of me writing down my dreams, which piece of paper would have been in my back pocket as he was speaking to me that night—I was filled with foolish pride because I thought selling insurance was below me, as was my image from those I saw selling insurance, I said to him these words, "I wouldn't be caught dead selling insurance. Those insurance people don't make any money." Not my finest hour. To his credit, and probably under the influence of the cosmos, he persisted and said, "Oh yea, you would be surprised to know what insurance people really make." Well, during that time I was dating my wife. The thought of getting married did occur to me and I knew I could not provide for her with the income I was making at the bank. So, to my credit I got off my high horse and asked his advice about what I should do next if I were interested in looking into it. He advised, and the rest is history. I eventually left the bank and jumped into a sales career feet first. I've never looked back since and I've never regretted the decision.

A career in sales has been a godsend for me. It has changed my life and I am very comfortable and confident saying that it can change or improve yours.

The jump into the insurance sales business was a new experience for me. I was in new and uncharted waters. Today no one would believe this if I told them, only because they perceive me to be good and comfortable at what I do, but when I started, I was very afraid. Yes, me. Very afraid. This was a big leap for me. I mentioned earlier that I had a brush with sales of various things, but in none of those situations were I the sole breadwinner supporting a family exclusively through selling of a good or a service. Up to this point in my sales experience I was as a supporting cast member to my mother. I started in insurance sales at 24 years old. Prior to that, I had worked at the bank for 6 years starting at 18years old. When I took the job, I knew I was leaving the comfort of a salaried job for the risk, at least that's how I saw it, of making more money in a commission only job, this time with a new wife. We had just gotten married in June, while I still had my "good job" and now I'm starting this venture in November of the same year. The Bahamas is a country of many islands and as was my luck, I happened to find a wife who lived on another island who had to resign her job and relocate to my island to start our life together. At the time I started in sales, she had not yet found a job, so it was all on me. For a long while, I was driven by the fear that if I fail at this new job, I would have brought this young lady who was doing quite well on her own into my world to experience a life of suffering because of me. I did not want that to happen. I had told her of some of my life's experiences, but not all. To be honest, for a long time I was embarrassed to tell her or anybody else the whole truth of what my life was like. Very few people know.

So today when talk to people about pursing a sales career and I see their apprehension, trust me, I understand. But for many people who are looking for an avenue to accomplish the dreams they harbor in their breast, a career in sales, whatever you decide to sell—cars, real estates, electronics, services, insurance, whatever, —can be the ticket to get there.

Now, once you make the decision to jump in, to be successful, you have to learn and follow the rules. I'm not talking about corporate rules, yes, you need to know them. I'm talking about the universal rules you must follow to achieve success in sales, period. The title of this book is, "Make it Happen," obviously, the "You" as in You Make It Happen is implied. The first step to being successful is that realization and determination. You will not make it without that. It is critically important that you accept that your success is in your hands, no one will or can do it for you. Yes, along the way you will find many persons who will help you, cheer you on and maybe even make some sales for you, but to be successful in the career, you will have to take that wheel and drive. That's realization. Determination is when you say, not I will give this a go, I will try my hardest, I will do my best. Nope. Sorry. None of those is good enough. You have to say, I will make this happen. If other people can do it, I can learn what it takes and get it done. Now, in the field of sales, you can do that. What I will share with you in this book will get you there once you apply the information. I would not say that in basketball, sprinting or gymnastics, that's just me. My name is not Michael Jordan, or Usain Bolt, nor am I Simone Biles' brother. I know my limits, but in sales, yeah, I can learn that and do that. That's a "regular human" sport.

Early in my career, I made up my mind that I had to be successful and I decided that I was going to do whatever it took. So one evening, I had a meeting with my new wife, we were only married for a few short months at this point and I told her that

I decided to take on this job that is strictly commission based. I had not done this before and I was determined to make it work. Therefore, I will be out late many nights seeing clients to generate the sales I needed. Thank God she is a good wife. She understood and agreed to support my plan. Over time I discovered that I did not have to work so many late nights to get great results, but I did not know that going in. Later in the book I will share why I did not have to work many nights. It has to do with markets. The point I am making to you is that I made the decision that I was going to do what it took to succeed, not just "do my best."

As I got into the job, I realized that it was not so bad, especially after I had made a few sales. Meeting new people and working with them to get them what they needed was fun and rewarding. When everything is going right, sales can feel like magic but it's not. In the beginning, I was so concerned about not failing that I could not relax, step back and see the process to understand what was going on. I really could not see the forest for the trees. It took a while actually, years, for me to be able to step back and identify the elements of success and the components of each. That's what I mean by sales can feel like magic when everything is going right. What actually, is "everything." It is that "everything" that consciously or sub-consciously great salespersons put together to achieve uncommon success. Most people never have a reason to step back and analyze the process to identify what is that secret sauce that makes up this "everything". I think I have identified it and its made up of five secrets that working together gives everyone working in any sales endeavor the tools to succeed and go as far as their dreams would carry them. Those five secrets are motivation, mental armor, sales strategies, sales skills and product knowledge. There you have it. I attribute all the success I've experienced in my career to the mastery and continued learning and implementing of these five secrets. I call them secrets even though they are hiding in plain sight. They warrant the distinction as secrets because thousands, if not millions of people venture into the sales arena and fail because they did not learn how to incorporate these five concepts in their work. That is the tragedy. That is what I am trying to help people avoid through what I share in this book. You can be successful in sales, you don't have to have superhuman strength, be able to leap tall buildings in a single bound, you can be a regular guy, just like me and change your future through a career in sales.

The job of a salesperson is honorable and indispensable. As I grew to appreciate the job I do, I respect it more and take pride in what I do. For me that is both the job of selling and the product and services themselves. The job of sales is to bring value to clients. Products and services in themselves offer value, but often a salesperson is needed to deliver and uncover the value that a product or service promises. The world cannot make it without sales professionals. We are represented by many different names in the market. We go by sales representative, Business Development Associate, Account Executive, Advisor, etc., but in every case, our job is to deliver value to our clients through the products or services we have to offer. We are in fact professionals and we all should recognize that. We ought not see or present ourselves as hustlers and peddlers, even if we are selling straw dolls, conch shells and straw baskets to tourist from a stall on the sidewalk like I did for years. Even in that job, I was bringing value to my clients who were tourist walking by looking for a souvenir to take back home. I looked up the definition of a profession and by extension professional. A profession is defined as "a paid occupation, especially one that involves prolonged training and a formal qualification." This is why we so easily fit doctors and lawyers in this definition, prolonged training and a formal qualification. One of the reasons more salespeople don't succeed is because they do not take the path of a profession in their work—prolonged training and a formal qualification. If you think about it, what is the net effect of prolonged training and a formal qualification? Isn't it for the express purpose of being able to give advice or do a thing to generate a sale? Absolutely. Doctors may not see themselves as salespersons, but they are essentially selling their knowledge and skill from training and qualification. Lawyers are doing the same. I know that in the insurance business that is what I am doing, and that is what you are doing, whatever you sell. If more of us see ourselves that way, prepare ourselves that way, we increase our likelihood of succeeding to such a high percentage that success becomes almost guaranteed. Do you feel me?

Now, on our training journey as sales professionals, whatever our job title, sometimes that title is CEO, we cover the five secrets to success. What I found is that some of the learning is bound in textbook and manuals. You would usually find product knowledge and some discussion about sales strategies in that format, but to find the other secrets, you must engage in other learning methods, one is experience, or learning from other people's experience. That's exactly why I sought to write this book. Other learning avenues are through associations, seminars, observations, etc. This is where industry groups, mentors and coaches come into play. I have had my share.

For the rest of this book, we will do a deep dive into those five secrets. Mental Armor, Sales Strategies, skills and Product Knowledge:

For all of us, every one, our greatest asset, our most valuable possession in the quest to a greater and better us, a greater and better life for ourselves and our families is our dreams, real dreams, our aspirations, our vision of where we want to be and what we want to achieve, and yet, far too often we treat that treasure like a jetsam, we neither nurture it nor cultivate it. We let it sit and rot as time passes by then we speak about it as a memory and a regret. A famous writer and preacher, Myles Monroe said, "The wealthiest place in the world is not the gold mines of South America or the oil fields of Iraq or Iran. They are not the diamond mines of South Africa or the banks of the world. The wealthiest place on the planet is just down the road. It is the cemetery. There lie buried companies that were never started, inventions that were never made, bestselling books that were never written, and masterpieces that were never painted. In the cemetery is buried the greatest treasure of untapped potential."

Don't let that be you. Your dreams are what will drive your motivation to achieve great heights in sales. Everything happens because someone was motivated to do something. Motivation is not industry specific, but especially in the sales industry we need to maintain a motivation level that gets us out of bed every morning even though the day before was brutal. That is the challenge. How we do that is what we will discuss because if we do not have enough motivation to overcome inertia, the knowledge, skills, strategies we have and know will not be deployed. That is why motivation is the most important secret we need to cultivate as professionals.

In this book, we will discuss how to cultivate those dreams, how to light a fire under you to get up every day and give one more push. We will discuss how to develop goals that will act as a guide post on the way to your destination and how to create a plan to achieve those goals.

Then with plans in hand, we must prepare mentally to face a brutal world. There, the romantic notion of a dream runs into the cold brick wall of resistance and rejection. It is only those who are mentally prepared for that who will succeed. **That's the second secret to success in sales**. Mental Armor refers to the mindset or way of thinking that protects you against the inevitable negatives and challenges that are inherent in a sales career. Also, mental armor refers to the attitudinal disposition that makes you attractive to your clients as well as puts you in the best frame of mind to take advantage of opportunities that present themselves in your day to day experience. We discuss in depth the elements of mental armor.

Mike Tyson said, "Everyone has a plan until they get punched in the face." Well my friend, I have to tell you, if you are in sales, that punch in the face will come. How will you handle it? We will discuss how to develop a thick mental armor that allows you to survive and thrive in that cold world. We discuss how to develop and maintain the winning attitude, mental toughness and professional aggressiveness needed to stand up to the cold world. Your motivation will keep you going, but your mental armor will determine how often and how fast you get up when you are knocked down.

The third secret I learned while I sold cars to get through college is that you have to have effective sales strategies. Even though I did reasonably well selling cars—I sold 17 cars in a month and got my name on the plaque for "Salesman of the month"—I was not the top commission earner. That honor went to another guy named Michael. All of the salesman would gasp in awe of some of the deals this guy would put together. He was the king of big cases. He would make thousands of dollars on one car deal when most of us had to sell ten cars to make what he made. The first time I saw him do that, I thought it was luck. Then he did it again, then again. Well, it wasn't luck any more, and we all had to come to accept that. So, I studied him and interestingly enough, when I left college and the car business, and got into the insurance business, I applied the strategies I learned from Michael, and next thing I knew people were referring to me as the "Big Case Writer." Ready, aim, fire. That is the correct approach to addressing a project, but too many sales people operate from the ready, fire, aim approach and as a result spend an inordinate amount of time firing and not hitting because their aim is off. In our deep dive into sales strategies, we will discuss how to create and execute an effective sales strategy that will get you results. In this book, I will lay out the strategies I used to get big results. They include how to identify your market, and how to penetrate a market. We discuss your value proportion and, very, very important, how to maximize your Sales Production Formula. This concept changed my life. You never go into battle without a strategy.

Believe it or not, one of the key reasons why people fail in sales is because they do not have adequate Sales skills. That is why having effective sales skills is really one of the secrets to success. I know. It shouldn't be. You would think people who embark in the sales career would have those skills, but clearly that is not the case. In the article I mention earlier from Rathbone Results, it mentions a Harvard business Reviews study from 1964 which stated that "A very high proportion of those engaged in selling cannot sell." Much has not changed. People often think that you have to be a good talker to be a great sales person and that "good talking" is a sales skill in itself. Well, if good talking means just talking, then the answer is no. If good talking means talking that systemically brings value to a client and walk them, hand holding, through the sales process, then, yes. I'll go with that. We spend a great deal of time drilling down into sales skills so that at the end of this book, you will know how to make a sale. I will share with you methods that have worked well for me over the past 30 years and counting.

Together, we will spend considerable time discussing the anatomy of sales, the perspective of a sales engagement from a buyer and a seller's point of view. We discuss each of the 10 steps in the steps to a sale and explain how to do each one right, including prospecting, fact finding, discovery agreement, solution design, presentation and close. We will also discuss what the common objections are when selling anything and how to handle each one. We even discuss how to set yourself up for continued success by showing you how to get quality referrals.

The fifth secret to success in sales is having the requisite knowledge about your product or service. This is a secret because so many salespersons think that the product or service is what they are actually selling. This is a huge misnomer. Nobody buys a product or a service. Products and services are manifestations of what people are actually buying. In the end people are buying a solution to a problem, prestige, savings, efficiency, etc. usually people are buying an intangible. Every sales engagement is about a product or service. Having the knowledge about what that product or service does and does not do is vital. In every sales encounter we are all, regardless of what we are selling, actually just selling one thing, satisfaction. To achieve that we must take the time to learn what our product or service does or can do and how that can bring satisfaction to a client.

In this book we discuss what features and benefits of what you sell that you need to know and know how to match them with your client's needs and wants to give them that intangible they are looking for. We will discuss what it is that your product or service can do to bring value, under what conditions does it work and how your service and delivery capabilities may seal the deal. Further, with respect to product knowledge, we will discuss what level of technical knowledge is appropriate for you to have to be good at sales.

You know, each of these secrets is a secret out there on its own in plain sight. I would venture to say that if you mention these five areas as components to a successful sales career to anyone in sales, they would agree on each point. The question then is why do so many salespersons either fail at the job or are not experiencing high levels of sales and income? What really makes the difference between that high flyer really successful salesperson, the one we all admire and sometimes envy. Is there some other secret the others don't know? Well, yes and no. Trust me, there is no other element to the package of components required to be successful. This is it. So no, in that sense, there is no missing piece. But yes, what they know and what they practice that makes them so successful is the biggest secret of all and that is this, they work each of these secrets together like a symphony. In this case, the whole is greater than the parts separately. I have seen over and over again where a salesperson, and I've hired many of them in my day, is strong in one or two areas but weak in the other areas, and just cannot put it together. This is really an all or nothing proposition. I would be misleading you if I did not disclose that. The great news is that in this book, we show you how to put the whole package together.

Each of these five secrets are broad sections which we will develop in supporting chapters below them, but they are not islands in themselves. To be successful in a sales career, you really have to operate them like a hand in glove. The hand and the glove are district entities but they are most effective for the right job when they work together. That is the greatest secret of all.

CHAPTER 2

Cultivate Your Dreams

Take a look around you. Go ahead. Go outside and take a good look around. Everything you see that is manmade is the result of a dream. But even more than that, it's the result of a dream acted upon. Dreams are your birthright. You, yes, you, are entitled to them, and best of all, they are free. You can dream as big and as long as you like. There is never a charge. That's what is so wonderful. Further, what is amazing is that, that same free dream that you conjure up in your mind can and has changed the future of the world. It is dreams just like that that created the world we live in today. What we see around us is a testament to the fact that something as free as a dream, when acted upon can create the world and in the same way your dreams can create a new world for you.

So let's talk about your dreams. What dreams do you have that will make a mark in your world, in the whole world? I believe we all have dreams, like I said, it's our birthright. How can you tell? Listen to children, "That's my house, that's my car,". "I want to be a Fireman when I grow up"; "I want to be this, and do that and have that" etc. It's who we are. As we moved into our teens and young adult years, oh man, there is so much we wanted to do, you remember, we felt like the world was our oyster. Watch out world, here I come, especially now that I graduated from high school and college. I have all this knowledge and ambition. I am bursting at the seams. Don't you wish you could bottle that feeling, that it can be bottled and sold at your local variety store or pharmacy? As we get older and have tried and tried, and failed once or twice, or more, the dream seemed to fade into the chaos, hustle and bustle and drudgery of life. We need an injection, a new lift, something to light a fire under us. What we need is to cultivate our dreams. Yes, cultivate. I think we would all agree that the "acted on" part of the dream brings the dream to life, but I put it to you that the richest part, the most important part of a dream is in the cultivation. There are three components to cultivating our dreams that will be the focus of our attention here. Cultivating our dreams means to bring clarity to it. What specifically is the dream or dreams for that matter? Cultivating means to bring intensity to it. This is often referred to as "a burning desire", and finally, cultivating our dreams means to bring sustainability to it. A dream cannot be a flash in the pan. It requires too much time and attention to be realized. You have to be in for the long haul. For your convenience, I have created an in depth sales training course that will guide you step by step through the whole process of cultivating your dreams as well as the full five secrets to being successful in sales. It is all there to guide you. Just go to this link to buy the course. It can change your life:https://www.udemy.com/course/become-a-sales-warrior/?refe rralCode=BB9BFDB5627DAC896D62.

Cultivating your dream is a function in itself. It requires attention and actions to keep your dreams alive and vibrant. Let me share with you an example of how not to cultivate and a few about how some very well-known people cultivated their dreams.

During this pandemic we endured lockdowns just like many other countries. So, I was home, could not go anywhere, so my wife and I decided to grow our own food, an idea that is much the rage here these days. So, when we were allowed to go out for a brief period, I bought some seeds, soil and plastic planters to start the seeds. We got tomatoes, broccoli, carrots, lettuce, you know, the usual and I got home and we were all excited to grow our own food. Now there is something that you need to know about me. I am a city boy. In my world, vegetables come from the food store, not the ground. This was a really new venture for me and my wife, but we had good intentions. To start, we put the soil in the planter, about half way, sprinkle in some seeds, topped it off with some more soil, watered and left it to do its thing. In the beginning, we would look at those pots every day, there were ten of them. For days, probably a week or two, nothing happened. Our energy and excitement started to wane. Really who can maintain that level of excitement. So we started to forget to water the plants. I would come home from work and ask, did anybody water the plants? Silence! Deafening silence. I would sigh and get water for the plants. Well, despite our inconsistencies, the plants popped. My God, the thrill was back. We are growing our own food! They grew for a while, we are still on again off again with our watering consistency. Then we got to the point where we had to take the next step which was to transfer them out of the pots and into the ground. Well, before we got to that point, they started to die out. We were puzzled, so we brought in a friend who had a successful garden. We learned that we had put too many seeds in the pot and each seed was fighting for resources and eventually we got discouraged and they all withered. Now we have to start the process all over again. This is how not to cultivate.

Now here is a great story about cultivating and one that turned out great for the cultivator and the world. I'm sure you're heard about Fred Smith and the story of Federal Express better known as FedEx. As the story goes, Smith found out about how shipping of small packages was being done in the United States. Shippers would use trucks or passenger planes to move the packages. He had a better idea. His idea was to have control of the whole process using his own planes, not passenger planes, to get items to their destination quicker. Now, stop for a minute and think about this. Put yourself in Fred Smith's shoes, no, let's put ourselves in his mind. When he started to develop the idea, what did he do to cultivate it. Keep in mind, he was a student at Yale when the idea came to him. He had to keep it alive and hot while he was going to classes, taking exams, doing student things and for months, if not years, he had to nurture this dream, this free idea, in his breast. During this period, I would think he thought about it a lot. I would think he investigated the current state of affairs in the small package shipping industry. He thought about where he can improve, where he can achieve efficiencies and where he can make a profit. I don't know how long he thought about this for but clearly it was on his mind when he had an Economics class paper due. It was on his mind so much that he decided to lay it out in a class paper. As the story goes at that point he did not do a very good job laying out the whole process because he admits that he did not get a good grade, but here's the thing, when he got his paper back and his great idea did not get an "A" he could have gotten deflated and left the idea right there. After all, this is a professor at Yale, no less, who did not think it was a good idea. That could have killed Federal Express. But no, Smith continued to cultivate his dream. It had to be months later, if not a year or so, that he actually took the leap and started the company. cultivate your dreams. The first thing you want to spend time on is getting clarity. What exactly is it that you want or want to achieve. Or take the story of Michael Dell of Dell Computers. At an early age he was intrigued by the world of computers. So what did he do to cultivate that interest? At the tender age of 15, he bought an Apple computer, not to use it for its benefits, but rather to take it apart to learn about how it worked. Now that's some strong cultivating. Now, you would think that shortly after he would launch Dell Computers. Not so. For years afterwards he would have to nurture his dream, crystalize it, maintain it, protect it, before he actually started the company a few years later while in college. So my message to you is that your dreams need watering, they need attention, they need defending to stay alive. There's a saying that goes, "use it or lose it." That goes for dreams as well.

So let's talk about how to? Notice that in each of the examples above, even in my failed gardening example, one thing that was clear is what it was we wanted to do. In my case it was grow my own food, for Fred Smith it was move packages more efficiently and in Michael Dell's case it was build computers and sell directly to customers. This level of specificity is not always there in a dream.

Many people in life are paralyzed by indecision and lack of clear direction. Not knowing which direction to go in is as bad, if not worse, than staying put and not moving at all. Having clarity about a dream, a clear course of action, is really more than half the battle. Once clarity is established all efforts can now be directed towards making the dream a reality. Now, let me be clear, clarity about what the dream is is not necessarily clarity about how to achieved it. They ae two different things. Often a part of what makes a dream a dream is the part about not knowing how it is going to happen. That's the journey, that's where the belief comes in, both of which are indispensable parts of a dream. Before you get there, you want to write down what your dream is; you want to articulate it to yourself. In 2005, I, along with two colleagues, decided that we wanted to launch out and start our own insurance company, an agency in fact. We had worked at two different companies in the capacity of Agency Managers and we thought the time had come for us to go out on our own. We had a dream. Whenever we got together, we talked about being in our own business, running the business and growing the business together, but we did not talk much about how. I feel like we were in the "Fred Smith writing his paper stage" even though we had not written a paper, we had an idea but it was not worked through. So, key point here is to get clear on what you want. Write it down, share it with a few close family and friends and usually if you ae not very clear to them, their questions about it will help you crystalize it. It being what you want. During this phase of cultivating your dreams the practice of dream boarding can be very helpful. I may have mentioned that I sold Amway products and built a network marketing team in my early years. That was going to be my ticket out of poverty. Didn't quite happen that way, but the experience was invaluable. They taught me now to dream build. They exposed me to real life stories of people who, like me, were not born in wealth, but through hard work and determination and having a dream, they were able to lift themselves out of poverty through Amway. So, read inspiring stories. They taught me to dream big and write my dreams down. That's where the dream list that I mentioned earlier came from. They taught me to cut out pictures of homes that I wanted, cars, travel, whatever and put them on my refrigerator, on my bathroom mirror and bedroom mirror to sear those dreams into my head. I actually did those things, and over time they came true.

As clarity is very important to a dream the question is how can you improve it, how can you bring the dream into focus more so it is clear, so you can see it like you are living and experiencing it today. Well, do these things. Claim it, speak it, feel it and walk into it. One of my mentors, the late reverend Wilbur S. Outten, may he rest in peace, once told me that a vision is going into the future, taking a picture of how you want things to be, and bringing it back to present day. I thought that was powerful. Wilbur read a lot so I'm not sure if the quote was original to him, but it made a lot of sense to me. When he told me that, it was years before I went to that fateful MDRT meeting in Chicago where the speaker put a different twist on how to see the future. His message was, "You can create it today".

So claiming it is your first move. Claiming it means making it your own. It means feeling and knowing that you deserve it, that you are entitled to it, that it is rightfully yours. Claim it. It is not as simple as it sounds. Many people struggle with the notion of them being worthy of that dream. Do you feel worthy to live in that neighborhood, or is it just for the rich, the famous, the well to do and those of a certain class. Are you worthy to be there? Are you worthy to drive that expensive car? Are you worthy to be the top salesperson and get all that attention and accolades? Are you worthy to be the owner of your own successful business? Ask yourself, am I worthy? The answer is, yes you are. But you may need some time and work and a success record to actually experience it, but you are worthy of it.

As I write this to you, one of my long standing dreams is to buy a Rolls Royce. A fairly late model. I have had that dream for years and to be honest, I had put that dream on the back burner for a while, especially because over the years I have had the good fortune to realize some other dreams. Nevertheless, writing this book has put that dream front and center again. I am so excited. And guess what, Rolls Royce has introduced a new Rolls Royce Ghost for 2021, the "Post Opulence" Ghost. It's to die for. I have already printed out the photos and I will be hanging them in my office and at home. This is what I did the first time around when I got my home and my cars. But going through this process makes me feel young again. I tell everybody that I am getting my Rolls Royce. I've claimed it, and given the work that I've put in over the years and the strides that I've made so far, yep, I feel I'm worthy of it, but I have not yet position myself to where I want to be to acquire it. I'm working on that so please buy my book, which you probably have, thank you, and share it with others. A car like that costs worth of $400,000.00 and to buy it you need to have substantially more than that, but it's a great dream to have because it lights a fire under me.

I have already alluded to the other aspect of clarity which is speak it. Tell people who you know and love what your dream is. Get it out. Articulate it to others. That helps you believe it more and it encourages you to stay focus on the achievement of it. Also by speaking it you are giving it life. You are allowing the dream to come closer and closer to you. The more you give your dream life through your words, the more your mind ponders on how to make it happen. Here is a quote from author, coach and workshop Presenter Michelle Landy, "There is magic in saying your dream goal out loud…and not just thinking it in your head. When you force yourself to articulate what you want, it forces you to get clear. The process of putting words to it will make you move from vagueness to clarity. It makes you get real about whether you really want it or just "think" you want it. And best of all, hearing your own voice say your goal, makes it oh so much harder to ignore…and that's a good thing!" So speak your dreams to yourself and to others.

For those of us who believe in the Bible, and I do, and I hope you do as well, there is a verse, Hebrews 11:1, that says, Faith is the substance of things hoped for, the evidence of things not seen." Do you see how it speaks about faith as if it is tangible, like you can feel it. It just goes to show how powerful the notion or actual sensation of feeling is. This is why feeling your dream is integral to bringing clarity to it. But you are saying, how can I feel it when it is not here. That's the beauty of being a human being. We have the ability to transport ourselves to a different place, see and feel things that are not present and be emotionally impacted by things we think about. That's why we can think about a situation or a person that is not active and present, get caught up in the emotions of that thinking and start to laugh or cry, even to the point where real tears are shed. We can do that. In the same way we need to feel our dreams. Sit there and feel closing that big deal, feel being recognized for your accomplishment, feel buying and living in that beautiful home, enjoying your successful business and driving that beautiful white Rolls Royce.

Do some things to improve the feeling experience of your dream. Go to the room in the hotel or office where they give out the top salesperson awards, smell the room, see the lights, walk up to the podium. Feel the space, become familiar. If it's a home, go look at model homes, sit in the rooms, see yourself there. Feel the chairs, the appliances, the space. As you add real experiences to your dream they become more real and realistic to you. In the Bible verse I referenced earlier, it is interesting to see the word "evidence" as a part of the explanation of what faith is and the verse encourages us to hold on to faith like it's a tangible thing as proof that something we are "dreaming" about is real. "Feeling" the dream adds that element of realness to it. When we feel it our senses recognize it and we experience it like its real and more importantly the feeling aspect to our dreams helps us experience the dream in the context of us owing it. You feel the house like it's yours, the applause directed at you and you behind the wheel of the car because it's yours. Do not minimize the value of the feeling experience in the process of bringing clarity to your dreams.

Finally, my friends, you must walk in to your dreams. This is the natural completion of the process to clarity that you began with a free thought that you conjured up. At this point, after having gone through the stages we just talked about, you see and believe that your dream is possible. It's within the realm of "doability", yes, there's a journey ahead, which may take years, but you feel that the dream is in reach. Walking in to your dream is living with that confidence as you work on the actual accomplishment. When you are walking in to your dream you take actions that are intended to lead to the fulfillment of your dream and you take them with confidence, even if there is some calculated risk involved. You call that big prospect who we've been a bit nervous about calling, you ask for a higher commission, a bigger sale, more resources, you do things that without the confidence that you will achieve your dream, you would not have done. Why? Because you would not have been as driven, as clear about what you have to do to make your dream happen. Walking in to you dreams means that you keep that dream ever before you as you ultimate destination. That does not mean that you will not go further than that, not at all, it just means that for right now, that is the targeted point of arrival.

As we are all too familiar, particularly on long trips, there are often stops on the way. Those stops are sometimes there to get rejuvenated for the rest of the trip, sometimes they are there so we can check that we are on the right road, but they are there nevertheless. That's what we want to talk about in our next chapter. In this chapter we talked about bringing clarity to our dream. Now that we are there, the next step is to begin the process of working through the accomplishment and that is done with goals. Lets give life to our dreams with goals. Goals help us to have specific actions to perform and guideposts to arrive at to help us on the road to dream attainment. That's what we want to talk about next.

CHAPTER 3

Give Life To Your Dreams
With Goals

Now that you have crystalized your dream in your mind and in your heart, let's talk about how to get there through a career in sales. Actually, I do believe that it is through a career in sales that more people have an opportunity to raise their standard of living and achieve their dreams. In this chapter, we will talk about giving life to your dream. In some ways a dream is like the body God created in the creation story in the Bible. God fashioned the body. He cultivated his dream of creating man. The body, once created, was like a dream, something new, something real, something with great potential, but something with no life. It just sat there. God could have stopped there, and this is where many people in life stops. Right there. I've conjured up the dream. There it is. I can see it, I can feel it, it's real, but it's not alive. Then God did what changed the history of mankind forever, the Bible says "God breathed into man the breath of life." That was it. Man became alive. As the Bible puts it, "and man became a living soul." Friends, it's not good enough to conjure the dream and cultivate the dream, to bring the dream to life, we have to take the next step, we have to give our dreams life with goals. For our dreams, a goal is the breath of life. Why? Because the goal gives the dream the first step towards becoming a living soul, a living reality. I am reminded of the story of the opening of Disney World in 1971, five years after the dream weaver, Walt Disney had passed away. At the opening, someone said to his wife, wouldn't it have been great if Walt was here to see this. She replied, Walt had already seen it. He saw it all in his mind's eye. What an incredible testament to the power of a dream that was given life by goals to make it come true, and there they were together experiencing the coming to life of a conjured dream.

A dream without a Goal is a fantasy. A dream without a goal is a work in progress, and that's of, in fact, that is exactly where you want to be. Once you get to the first goal, you set another one. This bring us to a discussion on how to set goals and how not to. Goal setting is not rocket science. Truth is, it's really simple and straight forward but it's important to know the component so that you establish a doable course that encourages you and maintains your hope.

HOW TO SET GOALS

You may have heard about SMART Goals. It's a good acronym and I will share it here. But I will also mention a few other components that I feel are helpful in setting goals. SMART means goals should be Specific, Measurable, Attainable, Realistic and Time bound. Let's take each one of those points and consider them in the context of generating sales. However, there is application for just about any other endeavor. Once you are able to identify an end objective, then you can use SMART goals to help you achieve it. In saying that your goal needs to be specific, it means that you establish a concrete measure. In sales that is usually a number for a particular metric. It could be volume of sales dollars, number of customers or quota of sales target, percentage of customer satisfaction rating or some other sales related number in your industry. The specific goal can also be an income number.

The next letter M is for measurable. Even though the goal is a number, in different industries there are different ways of counting progress that accrues to you. In the insurance business there are times when sales you generate have to be split or shared with one or more persons. In the real estate business, between splits with your broker, if you are a salesperson, and splits with another broker in co-broke situations, you do not get the full credit or commission for a sale. So whatever business you are in, you, in your own mind, want to establish the clear bases for measurement towards your goal. What do you count and how. Also, on the point of measurement, I strongly recommend that you keep a score board some where you can see it regularly and should update it on a consistent time period either daily, weekly or monthly. Yearly, is way too long.

"A" stands for attainable. Each of the points in SMART is important, but I fee especially drawn to this point because this is really where the rubber meets the road. The juggle here is between setting a goal too high or too low. It's actually ok if you do either in the beginning because the greater rule is to start the process and improve or perfect it as you go, but establishing an attainable goal that is still challenging is the real trick. So let's say you sold 100 units last year and this year you want to set your goal to sell 200. Well, whether or not that is an attainable goal really depends on a number of factors like the kind of business you are in, the time allocation required to do that, the state of the economy generally and the conditions in your industry. For some people, doubling their unit count in one year is very doable because they know that last year they really did not put out the effort and still did 100. For others, they went all out last year which yielded a 100 units year. In that case a more attainable goal may be to do 110 units while working on other approaches to get to 200 like hiring help. The point is that determining that your goal is an attainable one is something to think about. Attainable has the connotation that the goal is not easy to achieve, but possible to achieve.

"R" stands for realistic and it's really a check against a runaway attainable goal objective. "Realistic" says "Yea, it's possible, but only if all the stars line up. Let's set a number that we can achieve if one or two stars decide not to cooperate." That's realistic. Now, no one can tell you if you are exactly correct or not when you set your target. Just make your decision on the best information and gut feeling you can and go for it. Having set a goal on this basis so far puts you a head of most people in the world. You have a goal and you have established realistic parameters for it. Good for you. Finally you have to set a time, a date by which the goal will be achieved. That's the 'T'.

The "T" point is critical because all work effort works backwards against that time. If last year you did 100 units and your goal is to do 200 this year, are you allowing the full twelve months or are we talking ten months? The time allotted has great implications, as we will discuss in our next chapter, so it's important to set a reasonable and adequate time period for the accomplishment of your goal.

A FEW EXTRA POINTS ABOUT GOAL SETTING

In talking about SMART goals, under 'S' specific, sometimes it is mentioned that the goal should be written. Well writing down your goal is so important. I want to give it special attention. Write down your goal. Like dreams, you should write out what the objective is and post it on a wall, write it on a document or stick it on your refrigerator, somewhere you can see it regularly. Another point. Your goal should be set in stone. Once you have thought through your goal on the basis we've discussed, determined to stick to it. Life is not linear so I know there will be many distractions along the way, but set your mind to stick to your goal. That is how you will achieve it.

One very important point I feel the SMART goals acronym is missing is "Motivating." Your goal should be, or better yet, must be motivating. Attaining that goal must be something that you long for, something that you can taste and feel the benefits of achieving. Is your goal to double your sales? Well, think about the additional income and the things you will be able to do with all that new money; buy a new car, go on that great vacation, pay off that nagging bill, spend more time with family and friends etc. Or, will attaining the goal garner you more attention and respect from your peers and your boss. Will your name be called at the next company awards banquet? Yes, the goal has to be motivating. It has to be what excites you so you get up and go. Nothing drives you more than an exciting outcome of achieved goals.

I have said this before, but now I want to make it a point. Your goal should be visible, prominently displayed where you can see it regularly so that its imprinted on your mind and your consciousness. The same as your dreams. For example, my dream is a new house in that really nice neighborhood. Take a photo of the house, put it on your wall or refrigerator at home. However, your goal on the road to getting that dream is to sell 200 units this year. Now your wall or refrigerator has two items, at least. Earlier in the book, I mentioned that I was in Amway. That was one of the things I learned from them and have used successfully. I did that for my house and my first dream car. I told you the story about my house. In my thirties, I needed to change my car. I was driving a beat up old Ford Explorer. It had seen better days. It had dents and it leaked when it rained. I set my heart on a new Five series BMW. I had never bought a new car in my life. So I started my journey to this goal by getting brochures and cutting out pictures and putting them up in the bathroom, on the refrigerator and I had a BMW 5 series as the screen saver in my office. They were up there for a while a few years, but I stayed focus and I set my work sales goals to make enough money to buy it. This for me was a very exciting and motivating dream, to finally be able to buy my first, brand new car. When I travelled to the United States, I would stop in BMW dealerships to check out the cars, get a feel for colors, features and prices. I know also that because I lived in the Bahamas, the taxes and other cost to get the new car in the country would set me back about $80,000.00 and that's real money because the Bahamian dollar is on par with the US dollar. Then the time came. I was ready to start seriously looking for my new car. I flew into West Palm Beach and visited the Braman dealership on Okeechobee Boulevard. I had been at that dealership a number of times just looking around. This time I felt so excited because I know I was in a position to buy. I walked in with confidence, asked to test drive a 530i. The salesman come out, we greeted and for the very first time, I selected a car, not to buy, not just yet, to test drive. I chose a navy blue exterior with beige leather interior. The car drove like a dream. I was all smiles. I left that dealership on a high. I had found my car, which I knew I could afford. Because I was on such a high, I could not go home. I got into the rental I came there in and decided to drive around to calm down. I drove down Okeechobee Blvd. As I was strolling, very satisfied with myself, I saw the sign for the new Infinity dealership. At that time Infinity was advertising its new "M". It was all the rage. Just out of curiosity I decided to go take a look. In my mind I was really all settled on my car. But, when I went in that dealership and looked at that new infinity, I was blown away. The interior was beautiful. An absolute work of art, from the seats to the dash board. I said wow. Right there and then, I fell in love. BMW has a great reputation for being "The Ultimate driving machine", and it is, but for years their interior was not the most aesthetic. I did not know how the Infinity drove, but I was sold on the inside. I guessed that that is where I would be spending most of my time and especially living in Nassau, Bahamas, I would not be speeding around that much, I would prefer the experience of the Infinity M35's interior. So, I went back home to the Bahamas, ordered by Infinity M35 online and in about 6 months right around my birthday, I took delivery of a brand new 2006 Infinity M35 navy blue with beige leather interior.

Get a dream that motivates you. Set a goal and put it on your wall. That stuff works.

Finally my friend, your dreams and goals should always be in line with your values and your priorities. Don't get caught working towards something that does not line up with your beliefs and who you are as a person. Always be proud of what you are doing and working for. All of that gives you a good feeling inside and makes the accomplishment when it happens that much sweeter.

CHAPTER 4

Develop A Game Plan To Achieve Your Goals

I think it would be fair to say that I am somewhat of a movie buff, particularly action movies. Especially intriguing are those movies where a well thought out plan will be executed. Its always interesting to watch the plan play out. I'm talking movies like Mission Impossible, Oceans 11, 12, 13. The Italian Job and I think the mother of all planning movies, this one is a Netflix series and a relatively recent one, Money Heist. Now, to be clear, I don't want to give anyone any ideas. Please, please do not try any of those at home, but, you must agree, when it comes to planning an operation these guys are good. Money Heist takes the cake because the planning was so well thought out for an operation that would take a long time. These movies shine a bright spotlight on two important aspects of a plan that we will discuss here. First is the value of having and thinking through a plan and second is what you realize you will need to make the plan successful.

Establishing a SMART goal is one step, and it is a very important step. Getting clarity about the goal is critical to achieving it and the previous chapter provided the guidance for that. However, if you noticed, the SMART goals process does not deal with the how to accomplish your goal. That's when planning comes in. Planning cannot be over looked. Pursuing a goal is too important to not spend the time to think through and lay out a plan. I had to learn this the hard way, but fortunately I learned it in time before disaster struck.

In 2005, I along with two colleagues embarked on a plan to start a new company, an insurance agency. We were all successful Agency Managers at one of the leading insurance companies in the Bahamas so we thought the time had come for us to branch out into our own firm. Seeing that our company would be a brokerage company rather than an insurance company, we needed to contract with insurance companies to offer products to our clients. We approached an insurance company about securing a contract. They were quite inclined so we met to discuss possibilities. Because of our experience in sales, we were able to speak very clearly and confidently about the sales side and the possibilities there, however, because we were not as experienced on the cost side, it was strongly recommended to us that we work through a complete business plan to incorporate all prospective costs and revenue lines.

One of the key points we had to negotiate with the insurance company was the rate at which they would pay us for products we sell. That would be our revenue and our margins come from our ability to control commission expenses that we pay to salespersons we hire. So we went back and spent several days laying out a written five year plan with revenue and cost projections. We had a rude awakening. The rate of pay from the insurance company, which we originally thought was generous, was actually digging us into a deep hole. With those figures, the business would have failed miserably. The planning uncovered that. In fact, seeing that our venture was new to the insurance company itself, they too, did not realize that the ostensible generous proposition would have dealt us a death blow, which nobody wanted. Once, through the planning, we were able to show them how the figures proposed were inadequate, we were able to renegotiate acceptable figures. After the first year in business, we produced revenue in the seven figure range and everyone was happy. Never underestimate the value of planning.

In my business I talk to clients about financial planning on a personal level for their family. It is amazing to see how many people have not thought through a plan to achieve their financial goals. In my presentation I bring to their attention a study that was done many years ago and is often referred to in life insurance and financial planning presentations. The study looked at one hundred persons starting at age 25 and assesses their financial position outcome at age 65 after forty (40) years of work. The study noted that out of the one hundred, only eighty made it to age sixty five. Out of the sixty five, sixty three of them had incomes below $20,000 annually and only three had incomes $50,000 or more. The old saying, "If you fail to plan, you plan to fail" rings so true. As someone who has hired many people in sales, I have observed the positive side of having a game plan in pursuit of a goal and the downside of just playing it my ear. That may work in music, but it does not work in sales.

VALUE OF A GAME PLAN
PROVIDES DIRECTION TO ACTIVITY

Having a plan is the most effective way to approach the accomplishment of a goal. You really cannot over emphasize the value of a game plan. In fact, in many instances the planning activity can be more time consuming and actually more important to the success of the exercise than the actual doing of the exercise. I have been in many meetings and made many presentations where I spent hours and hours, sometime days preparing, planning, anticipating questions, learning facts, thinking through what to say here, when to say it, what not to bring up etc. to prepare for a meeting that takes minutes and often less than an hour. But that's how it is. It is your readiness for that moment, your ability to answer questions with confidence, take shots that were not expected, make recommendations from observations that were not obvious and bring solutions that bring value. It is that sharpness and presence that planning and preparation gives.

The purpose of a game plan is to lay out the steps to the accomplishment of your goal. What you need to do and how you will do it. In going through that exercise you identify the critical activities that need to be carried out. Once the plan is set, when you wake up the next morning, what you need to do is set. For salespersons, our job entails a number of activities, some more important than others, but all are necessary to the job. I'm sure, if you are like me, there are things about the job that you do not like to do. Some things come easier and are more enjoyable than other things. Some salespersons absolutely abhor paperwork, filling out applications, filing, following through on files to make sure all the paperwork it together. Especially in the world of tight compliance, you really can get drowned in paper work; but its part of the job. Some things you can give your assistant to do but some you cannot. Others abhor the calling to book appointments. We all know about call reluctance. It's a thing. Then others still do not like the service after the sale part. You know, its not exciting. The sale has already been done and logged, let me turn this part over to someone else.

When you have a game plan for sales production, you allocate time for all required activity. In my business, we call that "block time." You block out time for calling, for interviews, for paperwork, administrative meetings, etc. This helps with managing your time and your emotions. Knowing what activity is allocated for various times during the day or week helps, really helps with providing clear direction to your daily activities. Spend the time to think through your action plans needed to achieve your goal and lay those actions out by day and week, I promise you once you do that, you will feel more in control and you will be because now you have a system that you can manage and asses as the days and weeks go by. This brings me to my next point.

A GAME PLAN CAN BE ADJUSTED AS NEEDED

A few years ago, we were pursuing a major client whose operations were on another island in our country. The Bahamas is made up of islands, all unique with their own identity. In the US, it would be like a large client in another state. The HR director organized a meeting for us to make a presentation to their executive team where the CEO and all the other executive level Senior Managers would be present and a decision about whether to go with us or not would be made. This was a big case so my colleague and I prepared and prepared. The whole trip was suppose to be just two days. The night before the presentation, we were asked to make adjustments to our presentation. Seeing that I was the lead, the lot fell on me to work through the night to make the adjustments. I worked literally through the night into daytime with no sleep to be ready for the morning. Shortly before the appointed time for the presentation, we got a call that the presentation had to be pushed back, then it was pushed back again. Now we are on day three or four and I am backing up into a flight for another very important meeting in another country for which tickets, hotels, people, everything was already booked and set. One more day and something had to give but these were two very important deals, and wouldn't you know it, that delay call came in. What were we to do! We were already in the hotel several days over due and now my flight was the next day and all the preparation and presentation information was in my head. There was no way around it. We had to adjust the plan and I had to give my very disconcerted colleague a crash course in all my preparations, thoughts process, power point slides, spreadsheet calculations, all that I took days to create and prepare, with one day's notice. She had to take the reigns and bring the bacon home. I tried giving her the old "You can do it" speech, "I believe in you". It was not working. She gave me one look, so I dropped that hype approach right away and got down to nuts and bolts. Fortunately, she is a sharp cookie. She settled down made the presentation her own, and closed the deal. That was a lesson in "be ready for anything." Truth is we had our plan. It was working, but things happen. We adjusted, but stayed with the plan to go down there, be prepared for the presentation, deliver the goods and come home with the prize.

In every plan, there is a list of activities to be done. That's another value of having a plan. Your activities are identified and can be allocated time and other resources based on a priority matrix. That priority matrix can be based on the sequence in time that things need to be done or on the value of each activity to the accomplishment of the goal. When I was deep into my sales role (these days I spend more time in the executive suite than client facing sales job) I recognized the calling to book appointment and seeing clients for opening and closing interviews were priority activities. I allocated the required time to them even though I know I had service work and paperwork to do. Sales work, even across different industries, is often quite similar. So I strongly suggest that you determine the high value activities and prioritize them.

Another Value of a game plan is that within the activities list, even where you have prioritized certain tasks to be done, a plan can highlight those tasks that are critical at a given time for the purpose of achieving the goal. Let me share an example again from my experience. In my business, usually coming down to the end of the month, when the company would close the books for that month, it was important that all paperwork, etc. required to finalize sales was into the home office in time so that those sales would count for that month. This was particularly important for two reasons; one, if the sales were not finalized that month, your sales record, that will be posted and seen by the whole company, would look bleak and you may get a call from your manager, and second, more importantly, seeing that I was paid solely on commissions, if those sales were not finalized, I would not make a good pay that month. So this was my life every month, but this saga was particularly acute at year end. Therefore, every year as year end approaches, priority of activity switches from new sales generating activity, which normally is the priority, to case closing activities to get all required documents etc. into the home office so those cases can be counted. When you have a game plan that you are working daily and weekly, you always know where you are towards your goal and you can see when you need to change emphasis on activities.

A game plan helps you identify distractions so that you can plan to avoid or overcome them. We are all subject to be distracted by that shiny thing; whatever it is. You arrive at work ready to begin your day and someone walks in your office and wants to talk about that game last night, or a news story breaks and everyone is around the radio or TV, or someone calls and asks for some document that is not critical for you at the moment and can wait, but if you give it attention, it will eat up your time and take you off course. This is what happens. A game plan can help you stay on track. When those distractions happen, as they invariably will, it is then that you turn to your activities list for that day and the block time you have allocated and remind yourself to stay on course. What can be helpful as well is to in fact tell people, "hey, I have this set out to do at this time, can we talk later?" "Can I get the document for you later?" "It is ok if I get that done after this time?" Having your game plan laid out can really help you deal with distractions.

Set daily targets to achieve daily "to do" list. Even today, I make a list of the things I want to get done that day and I check things off as they are done. Yes, there are days I don't get everything completed, so I just add them on to the next day's list. I find that if I don't do that my day can go haywire for lack of clear direction. When I am working with my list, I feel in control and especially those days when I am able to check off everything, I go home feeling accomplished and feeling that I am moving in the right direction towards y goal. So I recommend that you set daily targets of things to do that are activities that will help you achieve your goals. For example, if you are in sales, you should know that sales is about activity and skill. The activity part requires the doing of certain things in enough quantity that would yield a desired result. Therefore, the number of calls is important, the number of client interviews, the number of referrals you get, the number of service calls, etc. All their "numbers" create opportunity for targets to be set to form your daily targets list in various areas. That is what you focus on getting through during the day. Your daily "to do" list is made up of activities to be completed and your targets of how much of an activity you want to hit in that day. This is a great way to set a course to hit a goal. Having that in front of you makes it easier to focus. Finally, with such a game plan in place it is very easy to go back each day or week to count up how much activity you did and keep track of your progress and more importantly to analyze your outcomes. When I was an active salesperson, every Friday at end of day I would count up my activity, appointments booked kept, opening appointments, closing appointments, sales closed and my ratios. When I began as Branch Manager, I would have my sales reps record their activity and we would use their outcomes as the basis of our analysis of their strengths and weakness and how they should set their activities for the upcoming week.

THE GAME PLAN MAY REQUIRE HEW RESOURCES

One of the things that laying out a game plan does that is extremely important is bring you face to face with the question, "What ae you going to do differently?" Clearly the reason you develop a game plan is to increase sales either dollars or units and or improve markedly in some other way. That growth, that improvement begs the question, "What will you change?" This is where the rubber meets the road, where we get out of the clouds and hit the streets. To achieve at higher heights a game plan will require new learning, new markets, new strategies, new efforts. I realized this early on in my professional sales career in the insurance business.

I started in the business in November of 1990. I had no degrees, only a high school education and very little business experience. My only sales experience up to that point was selling straw work to tourist, souvenirs, and sea shells. The Manager of a local insurance company decided to take a chance on me as a sales representative in his branch. I knew nothing about insurance, how to sell it our even why people would want to buy it. I had no market, or so I thought. For the first year, I worked quite inefficiently. I did not know how to target a market, the people I did approach were from all kinds of different backgrounds. I struggled trying to answer questions that some clients would raise, as I think about it, I really was like a loose cannon, I was not polished, educated in my field, nor confident. I was not a professional. After a year in the business, I recognized that and decided that I needed new learning to polish me up. With that new learning, I would be more able to approach and serve new markets. So, I quit my job and went to university. For four years I studied business, got a Bachelor's degree in Business and came back in the business and later I got an MBA. Using my new found knowledge that gave me confidence, I was able to penetrate the professional market. I felt comfortable dealing with lawyers, doctors, architects, engineers and bankers. I was able to hone in on an effective strategy and that made all the difference. Now I moved from being a loose cannon to a guided missile. I applied new effort, more calls, appointments, etc. to my new strategy and for the first time in my young life, I was making a six figure income. Life began to change.

CHAPTER 5

Put On Your Armor

In sales, as in life, your attitude is ultra-important. I'm sure you have heard the saying, "Your attitude determines your altitude." It sounds corny, but believe that. Its true. The right attitude is especially required in a sales career. Too many things can and do go wrong. Quite often, your attitude is really all you have to lean on; your point of view, the way you handle rejection, how you take bad news and the way you think about hard work. Because I understand how the term "right attitude" can be vague, let me spell it out here so that there is no ambiguity. You need to be clear on what the right attitude is. The right attitude is a winning attitude, one with mental toughness, an attitude that feeds your motivation for action and an attitude where your critical beliefs are deepen. With this disposition as a part of your mental preparedness, you are then able to Armor up with certain attitudinal mindset to greatly increase your chances of success in sales.

When you mention the idea of "a winning attitude" to people it sounds like fluff. They think its about smiling all the time, being friendly and optimistic. Well, that's not what I mean. When I say you need to have a winning attitude, I mean an attitude that will get you to win in the game of sales. That attitude has these elements. Someone with a winning attitude has a hunger for success. They are always looking out for an opportunity and they are ready to pounce when it is in sight. When I was a young salesman several of us were situated in a "bull pen," where our cubicles were near to each other. From time to time, a call would come in over the PA system that a walk in client was at the front desk and a salesperson was needed to assist. You would think there would be a mad rush to the front desk to get that client, but no. Some of those salespersons would just sit there like they didn't hear it. I would get up every time. That's hunger. You have got to be hungry. If you are somewhere and someone expresses some interest in your product or service or appears to have a need or need a solution, even if they are not directly talking to you, if appropriate, you would make an effort to slip that person a card or introduce yourself in some way. That's being hungry. There is nothing wrong with being hungry. Then you have to hustle. Some people will take a year and a Sunday to get done something that can be done in a day. In sales, you appreciate that time is money, the sooner you can get this case wrapped up, the sooner you can log your commissions or sale and go out and get another one. Again, time is money. The right attitude is understanding that point.

Finally, there is one counter intuitive aspect of a winning attitude and that is you do not want to be a hound to people. No one likes an over persistent salesperson who does not know when to stop. I've heard the saying, I don't take "No" for an answer as if that is a mark of a super successful achiever, but the fact is every successful salesperson has learned when to stop. Not taking No for an answer should be true about your efforts towards your goals, but it should not be sure about continuing to pursue a customer who is annoyed at your excessive pursuits. So the question is, when do you know when to stop. I use two rules of thumb. First, when I am in the sale engagement and I get to the close where I have done all the right things before I get there (we will discuss these in depth later). I go for the close up to seven times in different ways. Sometimes, I don't get to seven, but I know that if I get to seven and its still a no go, I stop. Second, I use the tennis match rule. In tennis, your opponent is playing ball with you as long as when you hit the ball to them, they return the ball to you. Its like playing catch. If when you hit the ball the person just stands there or walks away, you do not have a game. The interest is gone. Pursuing someone beyond that point is hounding them. Don't do that.

Another aspect of a Winning Attitude is a healthy discontentment about where you are. I say healthy because the idea is not that you should be miserable. In fact you could be doing very well in your job, making lots of money and breaking records, but that very situation is evidence of a state of healthy discontent. We should always be striving to improve, be better and do better. We should never become satisfied with last years performance to the extent that we are not reminded to improve upon it. That's what I mean. But believe it or not there are people like that. They are not interested in improving their performance, and then they wonder why they are not advancing in life even though they had good to great numbers in the past. As a rule, nothing in life stays at a standstill. At any moment in time, everything is either getting better or getting worse, even if it's just vacillating between the two. A healthy discontent keeps us in the game and keeps as growing. I think we owe that to ourselves.

Consistent with the disposition of a healthy discontent, the person with a winning attitude also accepts that there is no place for complacency. You can always tell when someone is complacent, or you for that matter. There is no urgency in their effort to change, advance, take new risks. Complacency is like a shadow that follows us, almost haunting us, as we move about. It seeks to come over us, make us feel comfortable about where we are in life. If complacency has its way, it would bring us a cool glass of milk, some cookies and umbrella and a lounge chair and say, just lay here and relax. You've done enough. Although, yes, there is a time for that and, I admit, maybe I need to do some of that more, but living there does not help us reach our goals. A part of having a winning attitude is fighting the urge to be complacent and getting up after that designated time for relaxation and getting on with it. Goals don't achieve themselves. This brings me to my final point on a winning attitude; Single minded focus.

The Bible has averse that says "A double minded man is unstable in all his ways." The point is that with a divided focus, it is difficult to get stuff done. A single minded focus allows you to channel all your energies and creative juices in the effort to accomplish your goal. There is this concept of being "In the zone." It's when you are in the execution mode of some activity towards a goal and it seems like you have the Midas touch, everything is going your way. You hear it sometimes in sports. A particular player gets "hot" and his/her level of play just seems to be at a new level at that time. This is the effect of single minded focus. I remember in Basketball, there was a season when during a game or two, or a certain period, Jeremy Lin rose to stardom. During that period, he played so good for a young Asian-American player, people thought that it was insane, so much so that they coined a new term to describe his level of play. They called it Linsanity. They even made a movie out of it. That's what single minded focus can do.

Your Armor requires a winning attitude but it also requires mental toughness. There is no way you can make it in sales without building the mental toughness required to deal with the inevitable and unavoidable challenges and issues that require that kind of headset. The good news is that once you know what the elements of mental toughness are, you can work to improve them. I will share with you how I have addressed it over the years. The elements of mental toughness are learning how to handle rejection, cultivating fearlessness and being willing to take risks. On handling rejection my old mentor, God rests his soul, told me once how one of his agents came back from a client interview in tears, a grown man, because the client chewed him out for trying to sell him life insurance. The guy could not handle rejection and resigned from the business. I know that feeling, even though I did not get to the point to resign. In my case, I made my living on cold calls. I would call people in the professional markets that I worked who did not know me nor I them. One call I remember distinctly was with this well known accountant at one of the big firms. From the time his secretary passed me on to him he started to berate me about how life insurance is a rip off, we are doing the public a disservice, we are taking peoples' money and not giving them anything for it and on and on. Then he hung up on me, hard. I was not able to get a word in edge wise. I Did not get to say, "Ok, sir sorry I called you." Nothing. After that call I felt so bad. I was drained. I started doubting myself, my industry, my choice of occupation. This call was really getting to my head. I could not make another call. I had to get up, get out and clear my head. To clear my head I thought through what he said. I did not know him personally, we had never met, and he did not know me, so, first of all, I came to realize that I should not take it personally. He was not talking to or about me. He was venting. Then I addressed the points he made. Were we ripping people off, taking their money and not delivering value. As I thought about that I realized that that was not true. There was too much evidence around to the contrary, so I was able to debunk that. So through my time of reflection, piece by piece, I was able to restore my confidence in me and in my industry. That was a hard experience but in retrospect a good one because now, I can handle any rejection using that same approach. First, don't take it personally, second, reestablish my faith in my field. That is my recommendation to you. So get comfortable with handling rejections. When clients say "No, I don't want to buy," they are rarely saying no to you.

Now, sales is a process of engaging prospects and customers to buy what you are selling. Every person in sales would do well to practice cultivating fearlessness to increase their comfort level. When interacting especially for the first time with certain clients. Based on what kind of sales you do, your interaction with clients can occur at different points during the selling process. Sometimes you are at the very beginning where you have to call to book an appointment and have to suffer through the fears associated with that and other times, when you meet the client, you are totally comfortable, and it shows. You are able to interact without the fear of rejection, the risk of feeling incompetent or feeling that you are not on this clients level to talk to them, which if we are completely honest, is sometimes the case. When you are at a state of fearlessness, it actually makes the engagement that much more productive and beneficial for the client. You are both able to address their issues and needs without the layer of tension present. A meeting without the encumbrance of fear is what you want always. One time I called on the Managing Director of a major accounting firm. As I mentioned, I focused on certain professional groups. This time the reception was much different. The MD agreed to the appointment. At that time, I was still young and young in the business. I called him because his name was on my list. I did not, in my mind, think pass the point of calling him. I had made no plans or gave any thought to the prospect that he would actually give me the appointment. But he did, so I had to show up. I remember arriving at the building and standing in front of the elevator. I asked myself, are you really going to do this? What are you going to say to this guy who is so much older and so much more accomplished than you are. After all he is the head of an accounting firm. Remember how that last conversation went with the other accountant. Anyway, I pressed the button and soon I was at the door of his office. When I entered the office, the space alone intimidated me. We were high up in the building and the reception area had a view of the island overlooking the harbor. It was breath taking. I could not figure out what I, little old me, could share with this senior man to get him to buy anything from me. I really felt like turning around, saying to the receptionist, sorry, I got the wrong office, and running to safety. But, cultivating fearlessness, I stayed. Shortly afterwards she called him and soon we were in the board room. Just me and him. I'm sure he could tell I was nervous. I could not get my usual presentation out, I did not know where to start, I was clumsy and my lack of comfort was clearly evident. I'm actually a little embarrassing talking about it now. But, to my benefit, I stuck it out. Finally got to the point where I asked for the sale. He did not buy but he was very nice to me and did not take advantage of my fear. He treated me with respect and we left on good terms. I could not wait to get out of that office and in the elevator. As soon as those doors closed, I breathed a tremendous shy of relief. I did not even care that I did not sell him. To me, the fact that I survived that interview in one piece was good enough for me. As I was walking to my car, I felt levitated, like I was walking on a cloud. When I got back down to earth and took some time to analyze what had happened, I realized that I had put too much in the interview. I elevated him to high in my own mind. The tension in the experience was created by me, not him. He did not bite nor did he attempt a bite. I brought this on myself. From then on, I learned. People are people. Don't make them more than that. Either you can help them or you cannot for whatever reason. Maybe they do not need your help, maybe they do not want your help, or maybe you just don't have the where with all to help them, but whatever the case is, there is no need to fear them. I was good from then.

A final note on mental toughness. Be willing to take risks. Let me explain in the context of sales. Every industry and market actually, has a way of doing business. Sales go down a certain way and clients usually pay a certain way or in certain modalities. In my business, the insurance business, most clients pay their premiums monthly, however, semi-annual and annual options are available. This is often the case in property and casualty insurance as well. Even companies for commercial insurance often do not pay the full premium up front. So when business comes in with an annual premium paid, eyebrows raise. This is always a good thing. When I got in the business and got my confidence up, I wanted to try my luck and venture out a little. Most people were maintaining the status quo and just collecting the minimum payment from the client. I decided to take the risk and ask every client for an annual payment up front. This is something I learned from my experience selling cars while in college. Everyone comes to the dealership expecting not to pay the sticker price. Everyone wants to negotiate. One day my manager said to us, when you sit with the customer, make sure to give them the respect of offering them the opportunity to buy the car at sticker price. Don't start the conversation with a discount. Now, I don't remember ever selling a car at sticker price, but the concept was novel, and he had a point. So when I got back in the insurance business, I thought to ad that idea to it. When I started to do that, believe it or not, every now and then I would get a client who would write a check for the full amount. So much so that in one case, I was selling this commercial client insurance for all of his properties. The value of the assets was over $10 million. The premium was very high, but in my usual way I asked if he could pay an annual premium. It was risky, but what did I have to lose? To my surprise, the client gave me a check for the full premium $201,000.00 plus. The risk paid off.

So in your sales endeavors, take some risks. Ask for more money, offer the more expensive product, call the unlikely buyer, or just try doing that thing in your line of work that others think is a risk. Have that mindset. Over time, it always pays off.

Even with a winning attitude and mental toughness, you can get emotionally drained. It happens to the best of us. As part of your mental armor, to be successful in a sales career, its important that you learn how to feed your motivation for action. There are several ways to do that and I will share a few with you here, but what's important is that you identify what approaches work for you and to be open minded so that you try other methods because keeping your motivation up is important to your future. I was sitting in my office one day and one of the salespersons came to me for help. He said he was in a slump. He said he was finding it difficult to find new clients, make a sale or make his calls to book appointments. That was not good. To shake him up, I walked up to him, pressed his body against the wall of my office with him facing me. I got a pencil and marked the wall on each side of his head. Then I turned him around and shown him the space between his two ears. That's where the slump was and only there. It was in his head. He got the point and went on to do very well. In fact, he went on to become an executive Agent and then to Branch Manager.

In sales our mental state is really all we have. You may have knowledge and excellent sales skills, but if your frame of mind is not right, you cannot deploy those resources. So to keep your motivation high, try these measures. Read inspiring biographies. Find stories about people who achieved extra ordinary things regardless of what their back grounds were. There are many out there that will inspire you to be all that you can be.

If you like good music, like I do, put on some uplifting music to get your blood pumping and your spirits high just before going into that interview, or meeting with a client. Remember nobody wants to do business with a sad face and when people are looking to spend money, they are not interested in hearing your problems. You need to inspire them. Here is a good one. Reward yourself with something that you like after you reach a goal or make a sale worth celebrating or achieving an objective in your business that is noteworthy. I fondly remember in my early days, one month I made a good check, as I worked on commission. When I got home I told my wife I wanted to celebrate. I wanted to go out and get a steak dinner. At that time, just being able to do that on a whim was a big deal. I enjoyed that steak and actually the whole evening. Visualize where you want to be. Whenever you are in your career and in your life now. That cannot be your last post. You must, must want to move to a next step, a next rung on the ladder, whenever that ladder is taking you. Take some time on a regular basis and just sit and visualize yourself being where you want to be, being in the position you want to be in and doing what you want to do. This visualization primarily refers to career accomplishments and advancement, but finally feed your motivation by dream building. We talked about this earlier, but its important enough to mention again. Take the time to dream build. Think about the lifestyle you want how and where you want to live. What kind of education you want for your children, the home you want to live in, places you want to go etc. Please take it from a guy who have had some dreams, achieved some and still working on others, life with a dream is better than life without one.

Another point I want to make about putting on your mental armor is to deepen your belief in those critical things that make you your profession persona. I have shared some experiences with you where my belief in my industry, my profession in it as well as in myself was challenged. In those cases, I had to take a step back and assess my position. You really need to do the same thing, and you need to do them along these lines, in no particular order.

Your belief in your industry. Is your industry one that you are proud of? Are you in real-estate, Insurance, cars, Books, computers? What is your industry? Do you feel confident that your industry brings value to its clients? Are you prepared to defend your industry if it came to it? Then there is your company. Your industry may be fine, but you may have some misgivings about your company. If you do you need to work that out. Whatever your concern is, seek to have it addressed. In the end, you need to be comfortable and confident about the company you work for. Believe it or not, your feelings about your company bleeds through. Take time to learn about your company and the value it brings to the market so that you can speak with and project confidence when you talk about it. The next thing is belief in the product or service you sell. Do you believe that it brings value and that it is itself a good and appropriate value for money? Would you buy it? Would you recommend it to your wife, husband, children or parents? Again, spend the time getting to understand your product, how it works, what value it brings and how it is good value compared to competitors. Finally you really need to deepen your belief in the value that you bring as a part of the sale and purchase experience that the client has. Quite often the determinant in a sale is not the product or company but rather the expertise, the personality, the assistance and advise that the sales person brings. In my business there are many people who my clients can buy insurance from but they buy from me and they stay with me because I bring value in the form of advice, commitment, help in achieving their goals and just plain professionalism. You can and should do the same.

CHAPTER 6

The Mindset To Go The Distance

To make it in the sales business, you really have to be built for the long haul. Achieving and maintaining a level of success in a sales career is really a marathon and not a sprint. Over the years, I have seen a number of flashes in the pan. They come in the business, do very well for a year or two and then disappear. Given the experience out there in terms of the percentage of people who fail in sales in their first year or so, this should come as no surprise. If you are reading this book, you are interested to know what makes a successful sales person. Certainly a part of that success is learning and implementing the mindset to go the distance. Here I want to share with you five points that have help me to go the distance and maintain a level of success along the way. This, I'm sure, is not a comprehensive list, but I feel pretty confident that if you apply these points to your repertoire, you will do well in any sales endeavor.

First, and in no particular order, cultivate professional aggressiveness. Earlier in our discussion about the winning attitude, I mentioned that you need to be hungry, you need to have some hustle about you, but you don't want to be a hound to a prospect. Hungry means that you want the business and you are willing to show that you want it by taking steps to pursue it. Hustle means that you move with pace and energy in pursuit of sales to bring them to a close and move to the next. Hound infers excessive bothering or badgering the prospect after they have expressed their lack of interest. Professional aggressiveness, though, is a more refined and sophisticated form of pursuing leads and clients. Its findings ways to approach a prospect or continue a follow up with a prospect that is respectful, non-confrontational, understandable, creative, unique and engaging without going too far to put the client off. This is a delicate dance and that is precisely why it needs to be cultivated. The way that you can be professionally aggressive is likely different on a client by client basis, even through some common tactics may apply. For example, if you are a car salesman and the client was at your dealership last night, looked at a car, expressed some interest, but did not make a decision then. Well a form of professional aggressiveness may be to email some articles about the car the next day. Another idea is call to offer them the car to take to lunch or dinner, whatever your company allows. Tell them you will bring the car to them and pick it up in the morning. If you are in the real estate business, the client is looking at a home, but has not quite come to a decision but you feel like they like it. What about sending them information about the neighborhood, comments from other families in the area about the joys of living in the area. What about sharing financing opportunities that you have talked to prospective financers about that would get them to the payments they need. How about sending them a reduced price that you spoke to the sellers about after they left. If you do these kinds of things over a two to four day period after your initial engagement, these efforts usually would be appreciated, understood and not offensive. The idea of professional aggressiveness is still going after the sale, but with style and grace.

The same concept can be applied when you are courting a prospect or generating leads. If there are prospects you would like to pursue, please do not call them over and over again leaving your name and number. That becomes annoying. Get creative. Find out information about their business, their goals, their passions, like art or sports, if its not too prying and the information is readily available, find out information about their family. Send an article about something they are interested in. If their team won a match or tournament, send them a congratulations. If a family event is publicly known like an anniversary or child's graduation, send a card. From time to time if your company is having a special event, send the person an invitation. If you are able to determine that their company or his or her department has a specific goal to achieve and you feel your product or service can help, send an email or a brochure and then follow up with a call. Especially if you have been showing interest without being a negative pest over a period at some point it is not unreasonable to expect that the person would give you an ear, in some form or the other. To be successful in sales we must be persistent, we must be aggressive, but lets find graceful and elegant ways to do that so that in our efforts to generate sales we do not alienate people.

Second, wear every case loosely, no matter the size. You know, seeing that we are talking about mental armor, I can't emphasize enough how important it is to protect your head, and nothing messes with your frame of mind more than when you have a case that you've been working on, it was looking so good and then it flops, for whatever reason. Man, that can mess with your head. Stuff like that can cause you to go into depression and set your activity back for days or weeks. Fact is some people do not recover from hits like that and just plain leaves the sales business. It happens. That is why this point is so important. You have to wear every case, and I mean every case loosely. Over the years I have hung so much on certain deals. Many have come through, but those that didn't really hits you in the gut. Shortly after we started our insurance agency we wanted to diversify our offerings to our clients to include general insurance. That is selling homeowner, auto and business insurance. That area of insurance was really not our forte, but we say it is another value added addition to our line up and a new revenue line. We were mainly life and health at the time. I went out and found an insurance agency that specialized in general insurance and I met with the owner and we came to an agreement for my company to buy and integrate his operations into ours. We agreed on a price and we signed a purchase agreement to solidify the deal. There were a few weeks, not much, to a consummation date. I was really excited because in one swoop, we had not only added the new line of products that we needed, we would also be incorporating their employees with the deal so that the expertise and more importantly, relationships with the clients would remain intact. During the intervening period we were making preparations for the integration. As we approached the consummation date, I called the owner. His tone was completely different. That was the first sign of trouble. Immediately I jumped in my car and flew over to his office. In our meeting he gave me this sad story about why he could not go through with it. I was devastated. I had so much high hopes for this opportunity, how it was going to revolutionize our operations and put us in a position to do things that no one else in the market was doing. I could not believe what was happening. I told him, we have a signed agreement! That did not help. Even though I could have pursued the matter legally, for various reasons, I decided to drop it. That was my baptism by fire to this concept. Wear every case loosely. Once you are predisposed to that position, you will insulate yourself from the impact of those kinds of situations, which in sales will happen. If you are going to be in this for the long haul. Keep this point in mind.

Third, plan to see ample prospects. I believe that there are three cardinal sins that most people in sales commit and as a result do not achieve the levels of success that they can. They are 1. They do not talk to the right people. We will discuss this point in the next chapter. 2. They do not see enough of the right people. That is the point we are making now, and finally, 3. They do not ask enough people to buy. This point we will discuss in the chapters on sales skills. But on point 2. This point is under this section, The mindset to go the distance, because this really speaks to a mental block about the need for adequate engagement to achieve sales targets. I have watched people who were excellent sales people flounder in the business because they were great, superb at the customer engagement point of the job, but they did not see enough people. So even though they did well and closed when they saw clients, because they did not see enough clients the money they made from those they saw, even at a high closing ratio, was not sufficient.

I don't know of any industry, mind you there may be one, where you can make one sale for the year and be good. Well, maybe if you sell jumbo jets, super yacht or really high end real estate. I've never done that so I don't know, but I would think even those guys would like to close a few sales per year. Seeing enough people is critical, especially if you are working with the previous point in mind. You don't know for sure which cases are going to close and which will pull back. You always have to plan to see enough clients as a buffer. What happens sometimes is the mind plays tricks on you and tells you that the cases you are working will materialize so you can relax a little and lay off the pedal. Don't fall for it. Your numbers are not in until your numbers are in. Remember that.

Fourth, believe in the sales process. For the salesperson, selling is a process that has a beginning, middle and end that both side of the engagement go through together hoping to come to a successful end. The sales process has been around from time and memorial. It has been tried and true and have brought success to many, many salespersons who apply it. Believing in the sales process should be a part of a salesperson's makeup. By believing in the process I mean that there are steps to a sale that sales people should follow and have faith that the process will prove itself to them as well. Later in this book we will discuss the steps to a sale. We will cover ten steps. Each step is important because it moves the ball along a path to give a great probability of success if proceeded with correctly. Some people get in the sales business and try to circumvent the process. They do not want to do prospecting, and if prospecting is done for you by someone else through lead generation systems, it is still incumbent on you to seek referrals and new leads. Some people don't want to spend the time doing a proper fact find and would prefer to jump straight into presenting the product or service. Others breeze through product presentation and go hard for the close, a close that is not there because they did not follow the process. Then the prospect gets frustrated or upset and leaves and the salesperson blames the prospect for being impatient. If you are going to last in a sales career, become very familiar with the sales process, each step, and why its important. You will find that your success rate will increase and your income.

Believing in the sales process also applies when you go through a period where you are not closing as much or as often. This happens to everyone. In those situations, just check that you are staying true to the process. Maintain your activity and things will turn around. That's believing in the process.

Fifth and final, do not give up as long as you believe. There is a price to pay to achieve success in any endeavor. Sales is no different. The great thing, though, is that in the sales field there is a track record of how ordinary people who had a dream and was willing to work within a system selling a product or service achieved success. That really can be your story as well. It is mine. My message to you is stay the course. Apply the information in this book, put in the time and effort and over time you will grow into your own success. If success in your sales career is what you are looking for, don't give up. You will get there.

SALES STRATEGIES

CHAPTER 7

Aim—The Key To A Successful Strategy

If you were to ask me what's the one thing a salesperson can do to improve their performance, my answer would be, talk to the right people. Spending precious time talking to the wrong people is in my estimation one of the three biggest mistakes that salespersons make. Just so you know, the other two are not seeing enough of the right people and not asking for the sale when you do see them. In this chapter we will deal with the first point, talk to the right people. This will take some unpacking so here we go.

If you stop and think about sales you realize that sales is just finalizing a transaction of exchange of value where one entity provides a product or service of value in exchange for another form of value, money. The entity exchanging the money has a need or a want that they want to fulfill. That's a critical point. If there was a way for us as salespersons to identify all the persons who 1. have a need or want for our product or service and 2. is prepared to fulfill that need within our sales cycle and time frame, that grouping would be a perfect target. In fact, the set of persons who make up this group would be our target market. Imagine, if you could identify that group, how sweet your sales life would be. Everyone you go to would be a sale. The interesting thing about this group is that even if you are not the best salesperson, if you speak exclusively to this group, they would but in spite of your lack of sales skills. This is why talking to the right people is so important. Just by their predisposition of need and want they are likely to buy from you.

Now we all know that in real life markets do not present that way, but that is exactly why we have a job in sales and why this chapter is so important. Our job in sales is to determine the market that we want to work in, learn how to identify them, the people in that market, and find ways to get to them to let them know that we are one of the persons who have what they need or want to exchange for value. As you get good at doing that and you begin to operate daily only within that market your life experience in sales will essentially be as close as you can get to the ideal above. The fact is that the market you decide to work in really becomes a lifestyle. So in this chapter we will discuss how to identify a market, various types of markets and how to penetrate a market. At the end of these next three chapters on strategy, you should be able to identify the kind of market you have now, what kind you want going forward and how to penetrate it.

Earlier in this book, I talked about how I started in sales. I operated like a scatter bullet. I went after anything and everything that moved. I was well intentioned, but completely misguided. That way of working was really working me very hard. Because I did not know how to prospect properly, I would drive to a shopping center and just walk around looking for people to give my card to or ask them if they were interested in buying some insurance. As I think back on those days, I see how funny that was and I understand now why I got the looks and responses that I got. Please don't do that. Save yourself the experience. If you are in sales now and you want to establish a baseline as to what your market looks like, just look at your portfolio now or your actual sales in the past year to three years. Knowing where you are is important. That's what I did before I pivoted. When looking at your portfolio, (either current clients or past sales over three years) take note of the following points of data: what was the average size of your sales? If you have major outliers, take them out, either very high sales or very low sales. These are not your norm. For example, if you sell real estate and you made

100 sales in the last three years most were between 200k and 500k but you got one at 2 million and because you did a friend a favor you sold something for 50k, take them out. Mark out your average within the core. The same goes for if you sell books, security systems, computers, cars, etc. Then calculate your average commission, if you are a commissioned salesperson. What do you make on average each time you make a sale? Next, what is your number of cases sold each year, not over the three year period, each year. Then identify some demographics about your clients. Where do they live, city, state, what is their occupation in broad strokes. Are they professionals, lawyers, doctors, bankers, etc. Are they blue collar workers, white collars, etc. Guesstimate, if you don't already know, what their income ranges are. Some of you, instead of working with persons, you work with companies or organizations, you can take this template and do the same. It's a valuable exercise. This gives you a look see into your current market. Once this exercise is complete, you will be able to determine how homogeneous or heterogeneous your market is. If you want to work smarter and make more money, you want to move your market into a more homogeneous market, but of the type of clients that fit your ideal image of a client. What is that image, well that is what you have to decide. Ask yourself, in a perfect world, what kind of client would I want to deal with? Create that model. Once done, the question you now have to ask is how do I get to more of them so that one year from now the percentage of that kind of client in my portfolio or sales outcome is greater. What do I need to change or do differently. If you are relatively new in sales, what we just discussed, if you follow it, that alone is worth many, many more times what you paid for this book. Identifying your market and then working in it is so important that if you stopped reading this book now and just acted on that, buying this book would change your life, but there's many more goodies coming up so read on.

MARKET IDENTIFICATION

There was a show on TV not too long ago called "Person of Interest." At the beginning and end of the show it would show a group of people in a normal street setting. The show presents as if these people were being viewed by an identification system that would mark certain persons with a box around their faces and certain data about them would show up. Wouldn't it be great if we had such a system to identify persons who fit our market profile. That way we can spend our time efficiently by only approaching and talking to real and high valued prospects. Well, my friends, I am very happy to tell you that we have just that kind of system. It's called your brain. You have the ability to do exactly what that system does when you look over a crowd through the lens of your market profile model. Sure, its not perfect, but it does a pretty good job helping you screen out prospects who do not fit your mold. To fine tune your market identification system, you want to look for prospects who have certain things in common.

Common characteristics: You can apply your search matrix to any type of clients that you work with, whether people, companies, government agencies, etc. Is this entity in the industry you want? What kind of job do they do in the industry? Are they married? Do they have kids? What is my guesstimate of their income range based on their occupation and position in their company? Where do they live? What groups are they apart of? What club memberships do they have? What are their tastes in quality? Some people like high end others are not so fixated. Some companies have a certain image that they maintain, etc. All of these are reference points and windows into our next point of consideration.

Common needs: Having common characteristics is integral to classification into a particular market. Within this group with common characteristics you will often find common needs or vice versa, actually. You could approach your search from the common needs lens first and then look for common characteristics. As I mentioned earlier, I am from the Bahamas, but I went to undergraduate school in Oklahoma. While there I worked as a car salesman at two different dealership at different times. What was common between those dealerships is that they sold a lot of trucks. I was not familiar with trucks at all. I couldn't even drive a standard shift. I had to learn, but the point I'm making is that in Oklahoma, trucks are a part of their makeup. There are many farmers, truckers, oil and gas workers and the like that makes having a truck a required tool. Today, actually, many of them prefer a truck over a car even if they are not directly using it for work. So in the Bahamas a truck as a need or want is not as great a demand item as it is in Oklahoma. Seeing that I am in life insurance sales, when it comes to common needs, I would focus in on their need for life insurance given that they have families, reasonable assets to protect and insurance to cover mortgage loans for there nice homes in the neighborhoods they live in. I would also think they need medical insurance which some may have through their jobs, or not. If I were in the car business, I would see their need or want for an updated truck, maybe one for the spouse or one of the kids or even for their business. The key point here is honing your search and identification skills so that when you see a prospect, you can easily identify and separate that prospect as a candidate for your market. Seeing them through the lens of common characteristics and common needs definitely helps to narrow your focus. Finally, another aspect of a market that brings more cohesion to it is the high level of interaction that likely occurs within the grouping.

Level of interaction: In a solid market that is within your reach, it would be natural to find that within a group of persons or entities that have characteristics and needs in common, you will find that there is a high or reasonably high degree of interaction amongst them. They often know each other, know of each other, do business with each other or have some other kind of connection to each other. This level of interaction creates for you an opportunity for referrals and ongoing business. When I pivoted from the unproductive scatter bullet approach to the targeted approach of working with professionals, two things about that market stood out to me. First was the level of familiarity that existed among them, and this was not only amongst professionals in the same field, this applied to professionals in general. The doctor knows the accountants very well, the accountants know the lawyers very well, the lawyers know the architects very well and the architects know the construction manages very well. I had never thought about it before, but when I got into it, I started to see the connections. Often, I would find out that this accountant does this doctor's books and this lawyer is this accountant's legal counsel or that the two of them work together as advisors for the doctor. There was this bee hive of interaction going on all along but I never knew that until I started to work with them. This created huge opportunities for me. Once I did a god job for the doctor, he would not only refer me to his other doctor colleagues, he would from time to time refer me to a lawyer or accountant, and when I went to them on the doctor's recommendation, I went there highly regarded because the doctor was well respected and he was paying the accountant and lawyer for their services so they took note that their esteemed client, esteemed me. So, the high level of interaction within a market works hand in hand with the common characteristics and needs to establish a great focal point within which to build your sales.

Markets can be identified through the three matrices we just looked at; but always be mindful that there are several different types of markets. Markets can be geographic groups, social or lifestyle groups, occupational groups and a natural market. Lets look at these in turn.

A geographical market is a group that exist in a predetermined geographic space. A country, state or province, city, island or section of town. All are prospective geographical settings. The determination about which to use for your purpose is based on what you do and need it for. For example, in my business, the professional in a geographic area that I can reach in my car are more of concern to me than those in another country or on another island in the same country for that matter. Just trying to service that group can keep me busy for years. However, if I'm in the business of selling yachts, I may include prospects in the whole country or several countries, like in a region, to be able to capture enough prospects who are real candidates to consider. Once you establish that area, then you apply the three matrices to identify those who fit your mold.

Social or lifestyle groups are not bound by geographic considerations. They can literally be all over the world as long as you can get to then. This group is characterized by their common interest in social and lifestyle related practices. It could be music, art, fashion, partying or it could be going to church, restrictions on drinking and smoking, conservative dressing and the like. Their way of life that has commonalities makes them a market that have interests that are similar so if your product or service appeals to them, you can find your niche there.

Occupational groups is another type of market. This market, I know well. When I decided to work with professionals, I choose an occupational group. In doing so, I really got to know the issues and concerns of those persons in those markets. Many people look up to professionals as if they do not have a care in the world. The fact is that because many professionals are self-employed, either as a sole practitioner or as a partnership, they are business owners and sometimes business takes a turn downward. Because they are self-employed, they have to create their own safety nets in terms of medical insurance, life insurance and retirement plans. Through working with this group, I was able to get an understanding of the issues that each person or operation was facing and was able to provide assistance.

Finally, there is what we call in the insurance business, your natural market. This is made up of the group of people who you know now and are in your reach. This includes friends, family, colleagues, neighbors. What makes this a market is the fact that these people you know and you can discuss your business with them. Truth be told, we often recommend that a new person in insurance sales start with this market, which is fine, but the goal is to quickly move to solidifying the market that you create the mold for. Very few of the people who were in my natural market at the time I got into sales ended up in my professional occupational market when I pivoted.

VARIOUS ASPECTS OF MARKETS

As you go through the process of determining or choosing the market you want to work in there are several aspects of a market you want to take into consideration. As usual, size matters, as well as accessibility, approachability and financial capacity. Be careful not to define your ideal client, create a mold, for a prospect that is few and far between in your geographical space. So don't create a mold for an Austrian born American movie star with huge muscles and a governorship under his belt. Too restrictive. There's only one of them. Arnold. But you would do better with an American movie star or star with huge muscles or former governors. Get the picture? The amount of prospect who can fit your mold in your geographic space is important other wise you will run out of prospects. Then, you want to consider whether your desired prospects are accessible. I had a little challenge with this when I pivoted to professionals. I had no idea doctors would be so difficult to get in front of. If you are not seeing them as a patient, they are really not that accessible without some help. When I started to call on doctors, I always got the message that he or she was not available, they were in with a patient. One day I just by chance started to speak to the office manager and we got friendly. She saw my plight, felt sorry for me and arranged an appointment for me to see the doctor. From then on I learned the trick. You get to the doctor through his gate keeper, the office manager. They became my new best friends. If you cannot get to your prospect, then they are of no value to you.

When considering a market ask yourself if any persons in it is not approachable. Approachability is a key aspect of a market because even if you can get access to a person, or company representative or board or executives, if they are not willing to see you, you then have no deal. Some people are not only hard to get to, they are not approachable. They will not talk to you or give you the time of day. Accept that and move on. This is where I apply one of my lessons from the mental armor section. No deal is so important that I cannot walk away and find another one.

Another aspect of a market is financial capacity, this one may sound straight forward, but it is not. Remember I said that I pivoted to work in the professional market. What I did not tell you is when I started down that journey, I had a rocky road. I came from working in a bank when I joined the insurance busines so naturally I would gravitate to bankers. When I made my pivot, I thought talking to bankers would be easy seeing that I was one of them. Further, given that when I left the bank I was not at a particularly high level, I thought that the higher ups were raking it in. I soon realized that I was very wrong. I started out with great excitement to talk to bankers about insurance. I got a list from the Bankers Institute, and it was a substantial list. As I called each banker one after the other, I came to realize that generally speaking the commercial bankers, the preponderance of my list, were financially challenged. That was a rude awakening for me. So hence, my point. Remember to consider the financial capacity of your market model. Establish the base line income for people and entities that you want to deal with at a level that one would reasonably think that such a prospect would have disposable funds at that level of income. It does not always happen, but if you think about it you will be better off.

Finally when you ae thinking about markets, be mindful that two businesses or persons maybe in the same industry but are in entirely different markets. Let's take mustard and cars for example. If you are not a mustard connoisseur, you may not realize there are different markets for mustards, yes mustard. There is the market for mustards like French's Mustard, the wholesome, family oriented, blue collar guy type of mustard, the type you would find on a hot dog at the ball park. Then there is Grey Poupon. This is the mustard for the exquisite taste, the bon vivants, the high and mightys of the world. This mustard is found in the glove compartments of Rolls Royces, no less. Its not your everyday mustard, but both are mustards. They appeal to different markets.

Now take the car industry. They know there are different markets. So much so that each of the three blue collar car makers decided to create an arm that caters to the more affluent of us. Further, because they appreciate the distinction between the markets, they have given their affluent counter parts different names and they sell them in completely different locations, more affluent locations. The car makers and their affluent arms are for

Toyota, Lexus, Nissan, Infinity and Honda, Acura. If you did not know, now you know. The point here is that markets are important. Recognizing them and catering to their needs is big business and is a great opportunity for you as you move through your sales career.

PENETRATING A MARKET

Regardless of what business you are in, if you have to find new clients you need to have a process to penetrate a market. The very things that makes a market a good market to be in could be the very thing that blocks you out of the market if you are not accepted or are accepted then rejected for any reason. Those things are the commonalities within the market especially the high level of interaction between them. If you get a bad name, they will spread that bad news about you. Its natural they feel its their duty to protect a friend, relative or colleague from a bad situation. On the other hand, if you do a good job, treat people well and with respect, they will gladly endorse you to their connections. This is your in. Do an awesome job with the first one you connect with in that market. It really doesn't matter if they buy from you or not at that moment. You want to present yourself well and professionally, be very knowledgeable about what you are selling, do your homework to understand the client, their business and their needs. At your meeting all of this will manifest itself in one way or another, even if not directly, maybe just through your confidence and comfort level. Once they are good with you, you will get high marks in their report to others. At this point, you are starting to make an entrance. So the first strategy in penetrating a market is over time to build credibility with each person or company who gives you an opportunity to meet with or pitch them. People like to see preparedness and knowledge. They feel that you respected their time and you brought value. They appreciate that and they reciprocate by putting in a good word for you with others. Building credibility may take time, a year or more, probably more according to what industry you are in, but over time your goal is to become known for what you know. In this space, marketing may help some, but your best bet is word of mouth referrals and endorsements from satisfied clients. Another way to penetrate a market is to build relationships with people in the market. Preferably these people would have become clients, but not necessarily. Building a relationship and building credibility are two different things. You build relationships by befriending, assisting or otherwise bringing value to someone else. This goes beyond business but it helps business. People are more inclined to do for their friends, than strangers and they are more inclined to do business with you if they like you.

Help clients build their business. There is a saying that goes "If you help enough people get what they want then you will get what you want." I believe that. In that vein, as you seek to penetrate a market you will encounter many people who need assistance in their own business in one way or the other. If you take the approach to be helpful to them at no charge, you will endear yourself to them and when the opportunity arises, which it will, they will be happy to help you. That help may come in the form of buying from you or referring you. You can, help people build their business by sharing advice, suggestions, helping them with getting something done, shopping at their establishment for your family or your business, recommending them, helping them to cut cost somewhere or countless other ways that you can bring value to the person's business. They will never forget it and you will gain someone in your corner.

Likewise, another way to penetrate a market is to help a client achieve their goals in whatever way you can. Everyone you meet especially if you are pursuing a market of prospective clients, everyone is striving to achieve something. If you can find out what goals someone has, you may very well be in a position to assist. It may be as simple as connecting one person to another who can help. It may be getting them a discount on something or it may be lending a hand on a project on the weekend, without charging a fee. All these small gestures, done sincerely and from the heart will in time pay dividends.

Many of my clients have their own businesses or are at a senior level in their company where they have employees who report to them. Always be nice, courteous and kind to their employees, especially the gatekeepers. You really don't know how deep the relationship with their employees go, and you really do not know who has the influence. As you go about your journey to penetrate your chosen market, remember to show respect and kindness to everyone at every level.

Finally, as you move around, as you talk with clients, prospects, employees and friends, be observant. Don't just look, see something. If you go in an office and you see new furniture and decor, well, that could mean that business is good and this may be a good time to approach the client. Vice versa, if you see signs of trouble and if you have that kind of relationships with the client, ask if you can help in any way. Don't just look, see something means that you are always taking in observations to help you assess if there is an opportunity to make a sale or build on the relationship.

The process of penetrating a market is not an easy one step. It takes time. You have to gain people's trust and prove your commitment to your industry, your clients, your company and yourself to them.

We have discussed a great deal about markets and how, as a sales strategy, to determine, identify and penetrate one. This would be a good time for you to stop, pull out a piece of paper an write down the characteristics of the ideal client you would like your market to be made up of. What are the particulars for this client so that you are able to identify them or it, if it's a business, as soon as you see it. Write this out and think about where you can find these prospects, where can you get referrals or endorsements to them. Make this your constant practice and before you know it, you will improve your sales to them and the percentage of them in your usual sales activity.

CHAPTER 8

Put Your Value Front And Center

As a part of your sales strategy you want to have in your mind a clear understanding of what your value proposition is and be ready to articulate it as a part of your presentation to your prospects. Your value proposition is that combination of your product or service's offering that bring value to the client along with the value you bring as a part of the package. That combination of you and your product makes your offering to the client unique. This is why you and a colleague can be selling the same product, but the addition of you and what you bring in value to the client's experience can make the package that more different and valuable than your colleague's.

Understanding your value proposition really starts not with your product or service, or you for that matter, it starts with your prospect an their needs as wants. Why is that? Well, it's because the only value of importance is that value that can satisfy the client. If you are selling a computer system for example, the speed, storage and durability of the system is obviously valuable in itself. You can add further value to the package if you offer to provide IT service with the purchase of the system at no charge for a specified period of time. As a stand alone offer, so long as the price is reasonable, this sounds like a great offer. However, if the client does not like the name brand, or is not pleased with some aspect of the system then the value that you have presented in mute. The value proposition should start with an assessment of the client's needs and wants to determine what would bring value to the client. Too often salespeople try to get the client to buy their readymade solutions without determining what aspects of their product or service would meet the client's satisfaction by solving a particular problem.

In the spirit of putting your value front and center, believe it or not, this exercise of engaging with the client to determine their needs and how your product or service can bring value, this step alone often times would separate you from your competitors, even if they are selling the same product. The goal of sales, and what actually closes sales is not trying to fit the client's needs into the product but to understand the client's needs and offer the product or service or both together that would meet the client's need and bring satisfaction. So when we talk about your value proposition and we start by looking at what that value proposal needs to be from the client's perspective we have to ask a few questions.

What issue, problem, concern, does the client want addressed?

What improvement, outcome, savings, prestige, new sales, would or could the client realize with the value we can bring?

What loss, embarrassment can we save the client from?

What fulfillment, happiness, joy is the client looking for that our product or service can bring?

We can actually add to these questions as we first seek to understand the driving force behind the clients interest in our solution. Sometimes the client's not yet aware of the possibilities that our solution can realize for them and we may need to make a case for an opportunity to present our solution. Even in such a case, getting an understanding before hand of what outcomes would be of interest to the client would better position us in our presentation. Some clients, based on where they are in life may be motivated by anyone of the points noted above or others. For us as salespersons, to really be able to have our value shine through, understanding that is important. That may require some investigative work, asking questions, reading upon the company or client and otherwise digging because the answer you get could mean the difference between getting the sale or not. Remember, the sale is not about how good the product is, its about how well the product meets the client's needs and bring satisfaction.

Every client is different, unique, one of a kind. When you approach a client from that point of view, you see the need to be alert to those differences and unique qualities that the client has. The product may be the same product that you just sold to another unique client but the reason for that client and this one would likely be different. Given that you want to make sure that you are clear on the uniqueness you bring to the table. As a base level, what you bring is the knowledge of what you are offering. Let's not take this point for granted. Later in the book we discuss product knowledge, but le me say here that too often sales people are not as familiar as they should be with what they are offering. When I sold cars and trucks there was always distinctly two aspects to my engagement with the client. One was the interpersonal aspect of the client liking me as a salesperson. Was I respectful, engaging, nice, etc. Then there was the product knowledge, tell me about this car, part. The fact is, you really can loose the sale from any side. Selling cars and trucks for me was a new thing. I had to learn what an inline six is, a 357 engine, a dually, other car features like how fuel injection works, what is sequential multiport fuel injection. It was like learning a new language. But, knowing that stuff gave you credibility and built confidence in the client in me. So when putting your value proposition together think first about the value that your offering brings to the client. Why are they buying and/or why should they by this product. Get to know the great outcomes they can realize with your offering. Concentrate on these aspects of your offering that is different, bigger, better than what someone else has. The differences do not have to be huge, they just need to be an edge over the other offerings. Sometimes that alone would do. However, especially with an offering that requires or is sold through a salesperson, it is very difficult to separate the buying experiences from the salesman. This creates a real opportunity for them to be a distinct differentiator in the mix. Your personality, honesty, whit, knowledge, respect, all of that ads to your value proposition package.

As salespeople, we can find ourselves in situations where we are the only one selling a particular product or service. I definitely am not the only person selling life and health insurance, and you quite likely are not the only person selling what you are doing. If you are in real estate, cars furniture, etc., those things have easy alternatives for clients to consider. Sometimes it is hard to determine how you stand out. One way to get feed back on that is to ask your clients. Ask them, what did you like about dealing with me. What are some of the things that keeps you coming back to me. How do I serve you best. They will give you some very good feedback, and I bet some of the things would surprise you because you thought nothing of it.

Knowing your strengths is valuable because you can then accommodate them. Strengths both in your offering and in you. Show the quality of your product, tell them that it lasts longer than others, let them know that you have the best warranty in the business. All of that is good, but don't forget demonstrate your knowledge of the product when the point for doing so arrives. Don't forget to be courteous and respectful, they go in that value calculation as well, and don't forget to demonstrate your commitment to their satisfaction.

For me, I don't blast my value proposition to every new client I meet, but I make it a point to convey to them that once they engage me, I will take care of them and take on their matter or take the problem off their hands. If it would be helpful, I would refer them to other clients I have done work for and invite them to call the client. What is important with clients is that you manage their expectations so that you minimize if not eliminate misunderstandings up front. Be clear on what you can do, what you would have to look into and what you cannot do, or do not do. Simple, but honest statements in your value proposition goes a very long way. The statements do not have to be super ingenious or mind blowing, just simple and honest. If you are a car salesman, you can say "I will make your car buying experience hassle free and enjoyable." This is appealing because car buying can be very full of hassle and unenjoyable. I know. A computer salesman can say "I will get you the right kind of system that's right for what you want done and stick around to make sure everything works properly". Wow. That's wonderful. Why? Because those are the key concerns people have when buying a computer. If your value proposition is bent towards your product, you can say, "Our security system has backup power source and backs up to the cloud so you don't loose footage or power." Great! If it actually does that.

Every sales person should have a value proposal about themselves and/or their product that they can back-up, either with referrals, a demonstration or some other support to give the client comfort. Keep in mind that engaging with a new client is like inviting a person to your home for the first time, you want to put your best foot forward, be very hospitable, make them comfortable and at ease, then you can have a great talk about where you both would like the relationship to go. When people are comfortable with you because of your personally or your competence or both, they feel freer to share with you how you can help them. This is your opportunity to strive. Its been more than twenty years ago since I made a cold call to a doctor for an appointment to sell him some life insurance. We had never met before, but he was gracious enough to give me the appointment. I went down to the hospital, his place of work to meet with him. As I started my presentation, I did not get too for before he stopped me. He said to me listen, I do not have a need for what you are offering, but I do have a problem. If you can solve this problem for me, I will buy a policy from you. I asked him to give me the problem and my proposal to him was that I moved at the speed of business so I will immediately go and address the problem. I promised to return shortly with a solution. In that particular case, I felt reasonably confident that I could solve the problem. He was essentially having service issues with my company relating to some old policies that he had for some time. I got back to the office and right away, jumped into looking after his matter. Within a day or so I had the matter resolved. True to his word, when I got back to him with the matter solved, he bought what I thought back then was a big policy for me, but it was a small commitment for him. From that very small but important deed a long lasting friendship began that has been, I would like to think, mutually beneficial. Over the years I've sold him and his family many policies, he has referred me to friends and colleagues and I also help him with his business. All because I put my value, that I can solve his problem at the speed of business, front and center.

What is your value proposition. What is it that you do or bring to an engagement that makes you stand out and that brings value to your client. Think about that and leverage that.

CHAPTER 9

The Sales Success Formula

Any good salesman would tell you that even though there is an art to sales, there is a science to sales as well. Often when we observe or talk about great salespersons, we make reference to the art side of their manner of working, their style, the way they are able to talk themselves in and out of a solution. The "artsy" side of sales really is where the glamor is. But in this chapter, we want to talk about the science. Not so glamours, but truth be told, it is the science of the sales process that actually makes a great salesman. Let me explain. I talked earlier about people who I've seen come and go in the sales business, some of them did very well for a short time. The fact that they are not around anymore is more attributable to the lack of the science side in their game than the art side. Science deals with facts, figures, observation of cause and effect, determining what factors actually makes a change in a process, and that is exactly what we want to discuss here to show you how you can dramatically increase your sales and your income by applying the MEA concept. MEA stands for Market, Effectiveness and Activity. It was understanding this that caused a pivot in my sales career and raised by game.

In the previous chapters we talked about markets, what they are, how to identify them and how to penetrate them. The net effect of markets is that your sales within them yields a certain data point.

Earlier I used the example of you, if you were in real estate, selling homes mainly between the $200k and $500k range. Well, the average of your sales, which will be based on the amount of total sales and the weighting of the specific amount of each sale in your total, will yield an average market number of let's say, $300k. This tells us that more of your sales are likely closer to the 200k number than the 500k. Well, there can very well be a colleague of yours whose sales numbers fall in the same ranges, but her average is higher because her sales are more closer to the $500k number. Whatever your number is, that is the number we use for "M" in the MEA equation. Let's also say that your commission rare is 1.5% often broker fees. The "E" stands for effectiveness. Of the three components of the MEA equation, the effectiveness component is the one most effected by the "artsy" side of sales. There are a number of elements that go into what makes a salesperson effective, but the end result of those elements working together is that the salesman comes back with a sale, a win. Later on we will explore those elements but for now let me just say that they include personality, product knowledge, connectivity, and connections. In the MEA equation, effectiveness is represented by a percentage. It really represents how effective you are at closing a sale. For each ten prospects you engage with how many sales do you finalize, and, if we can rely on that ratio, then we can include that ratio (percentage) in our equation. That is your "E". You might be sitting there thinking, I don't know my E. How do I find that out? I'm glad you asked. This is where record keeping becomes important. When I was deep in selling on a daily basis, at the end of each week I would count up the amount of actual client appointments I had and the number of sales closed. This is how things operate in the life insurance sales business. When I sold cars, I did not really work on the basis of appointments, but rather on the amount of customers I picked up from those who came on the lot looking for a car or truck. The car sales business was brutal in that if you did not keep a keen eye out on that entrance to the lot, your colleague would quite likely jump out of his chair before you and head after that car as it drove through the lot. That's one you just lost, and only God knew when the next one would drive through. I don't know how you get prospects in your business, but you need to keep in mind that each engagement with a prospect in a given time frame, one week, month, quarter or year, counts towards your E calculation.

Now it's important that you establish the right bases to use for the calculation of your E. If you use the wrong bases, you would end up with a distorted number that may discourage you. During each week I would have two basic kinds of appointment with prospects. Either I would be meeting with the prospect for the first time to open up a new discussion about a possible purchase, or I would be meeting as a follow up to a previous meeting where I would have done the fact find, presented a solution that I left with them to review for a decision or I am meeting with them the second time both to present a solution and go for the close. If my meeting is a "going for the close", meeting, I would label it just that, a closing appointment. It does not matter what you are selling, in every case there is an "opening period", getting to know, introducing the product or solution, then there is the decision making period, "closing". Some engagements require multiple meetings. One way to assess whether a meeting is an opening or closing meeting is to consider what outcome do you reasonably expect to realize after the meeting. A meeting can be to clear up a question, but once that question is cleared up will the prospect have the information they need to make a decision. If not, then it's probably just a continuation of an opening meeting where they are still in the information gathering phase. In either event, we need to know how to categorize a meeting so that we can plug in that data point in our MEA equation. Let us tie this all together with a discussion of the last component of the MEA equation, and that is the "A" for Activity.

Activity is the data point for the number of engagements that you have during a period. So, in a given month, how many total engagements do you have with clients or prospects where you are trying to sell them something for the first time. This does not count service call engagements. This is an engagement where you open a new file for a new prospective sale. This person could be a current client or a newly met, first time prospect, but the key here is that you are discussing a new purchase with this person or entity. The total amount of engagements let's say is fiver for the month. Use whatever time period, a week, month or year, that is a common measurement period in your business. Separate the four into opening and closing engagements. So far easy numbers, lets say you had two openings and three closings. Now, let's say you sold one case in that month period. If we use the 5 total, your E would be 20% and you're A would be five. But, if we used just the closing engagement for the "A" data point, your closing ratio would be 33%. For the MEA calculation, you can use either approach, so long as you know what you are doing. Using the closing engagements give you a real picture of your closing effectiveness because you are only counting those cases where you had the opportunity to go through the full process of fact finding and presenting a solution. You had the opportunity to make your case. On the other hand, using the total number provides a quick and easy way to measure your effectiveness based on your total activity. Even though I think the closing engagements approach is more real and accurate, I actually use the total engagements approach because that one number informs my complete activity for the period and I know that if I get enough of them in, I will invariably yield some closing appointments as well. Of course the other sided to that is when I would go a whole week with only opening engagements. Obviously during those weeks I would have no sales as well.

Now that we have our data points; Market—average house sale at 300k at a commission of 1.5% or $4500, Effectiveness at 20% considering all engagements, and our Activity, the number of engagements at five for this period, we can complete our MEA evaluations and more importantly, do sensitivity analyses to determine the impact of improvements in the various components would have on our income if they can be achieved, and I believe they can. Here is our equation with the current information for a month.

$$M \times E \times A$$

$$4{,}500 \times 20\% \times 5 = \$4500$$

Let me translate this equation in plain English. This equation says if, during a month, you had engagements with five people on the purchase of a house in the market where the selling price and expected sale price was $300k and at your usual closing ratio of one sale for every five clients you see, your commission that month would be $4500.00. However, now that you understand these numbers let's look at how we can improve your income. Currently you are talking to prospects in the 300k range of sales. That's your average in the $200k – $500k market. What if, in your current range, you decided not to focus on any case that is below $300K and you now sell exclusively in the $300 – $500 range homes if you can, based on where you are, and your average sale goes to $400K and your commission to $6,000. Let's say your effectiveness remains the same as well as the amount if persons you are seeing. This equation can improve to this:

$$M \times E \times A$$

$$6000 \times 20\% \times 5 = 6,000$$

Just by focusing on the $300k – $500k cases and making that unilateral decision while not doing anything else to improve your effectiveness or the amount of persons you see, you have increased your income by $1500 per month, $18,000 per year. Some of you look at that and say, yeah, that's easier said than done. To that I say, yes, it is easier said than done. This is not about making it easier, it's adjustment. Making it smarter and more efficient. In this scenario the change is in the market. It requires you to focus on a higher market and spend more time identifying those prospects as opposed to just taking what comes your way. One of the hardest things I had to do when I pivoted to the professional market is to say no to nonprofessional prospects who crossed my path. Some of them literally offered their business to me, but I would refer them to a colleague. Most of the time I was so busy sourcing and pursuing my ideal prospect, I was not around to be found by a nonmarket prospect. So, yes, honing in on a specific market does require some time and effort. Now let's look at making a change in your effectiveness without changing anything else.

$$M \times E \times A$$

$$\$4,500 \times 30\% \times 5 = \$6,750.$$

Here you improved your effectiveness from 20% to 30%. The question is, is that realistic? The answer is absolutely. Earlier we talked about the art and science aspects of sales and I said that the effectiveness component give more opportunity to express artistic tendencies. Well, here are some ways that you can improve your effectiveness, this one does not rely on art as much, it is this: qualify your prospects better. The closer you can get to engaging only with prospects who are in the market for your product or service, has the ability to pay and who expresses or demonstrates a real need or want for your product or service the better a chance you give yourself for making a sale. On the artsy side, first thing you can do is be more personable and friendly. Don't be so ridged so that people endear themselves to you quicker and feel free to open up about their real feelings. Now, I'm talking about people and this sounds only relative to personal selling, but this is true about corporate sales as well because in the end, they are people too. Second "artsy" thing you can do is know more about your product or service. Later in the book we discuss the various aspects of products and what they mean and do for clients. Products and services have non tangible aspects to them that make them attractive to clients as well. Those are the kinds of artsy things you need to know about your product as well. Another thing, seek to establish more connectivity with your prospect. Is there something you have in common like sports, schools, neighborhood, family, friends, food, work, history, background, find something to connect. This opens doors in the minds and hearts of people. Finally, another artsy thing is to use your connections to find and make connections. I call these things "artsy" because unlike science, they are not numbers based. They are not hard and fast. They are more touchy, feelly, but you need them. After all as human beings we are not ones and zeros.

At an effectiveness of 30% with your market staying put at $4500 and your activity remaining at 5 engagements your income increases by $2,250 per month. Your income goes from $54,000 a year to $81,000.

Finally, let's look at the impact of activity, the other two elements remaining the same.

$$M \times E \times A$$

$$\$4,500 \times 20\% \times 7 = \$6300.$$

In this example, seeing two additional engagements per month can make a big impact. This component clearly requires additional work, but it may be the easiest of the three components to change. All it says is see more engagements. Let me add a disclaimer here. I have never sold real estate as a sales representative before. If you are in real estate and you are reading this, I don't want to over simplify your work. I have been in sales for over 30 years, but I don't know if for you seeing five or seven engagements is a lot or closing 20% of your total engagements is plenty. What I do know is that if you put your actual numbers in these slots and work them through with reasonable improvement projections, you will see how you can substantially improve your income.

Now comes the most beautiful thing of all. This is the realization that blew my mind and my income all the way up. This realization right here is a game changer. Consider this. You have seen what a small change to each of these components can yield, but what if you dared to make a change in each of the components all at once. What if you woke up tomorrow morning and said, you know, from now on I am only going to deal with this market, from now on I am going to qualify every prospect and employ my "artsy" skills to improve my effectiveness or closing ratio and from now on I am going to see more engagements consistently than I have done in the past. Wow. What would that outcome look like? It would look like this:

$$M \times E \times A$$

$$6000 \times 30\% \; 7 = 12,600$$

Your income goes from $54,000 per year to $151,200.00! When you combine the impact of these changes at once, the outcome is a change in your life! Your whole world changes. You walk differently, you talk differently, you ear different, you live different and you drive different. Everything is different. Trust me. You can now take that vacation and relax because you have money in your pocket. You can buy that new car, and this time it's brand new, not just new to you. You can buy that new house, in that nice neighborhood and when you see people passing by and looking at houses, they are looking at yours. That's what those changes can do for you in this humble occupation called sales.

The MEA equation. It is the key to unlock the door to a better life. It is really the sales success formula you've been waiting to apply in your life. I want to challenge you to try it.

Finally friends in this segment on sales strategies, let's look a little deeper into our record keeping and activity tracking and measuring protocols. I've heard it said that people think that sales is a numbers busines. Actually sales is a ratios business to be more accurate. As a salesperson you should keep or at the very least know and keep a mental ratio calculation of the following:

Prospects to calls – What that means is, how many prospects do you need to dial to reach one call? This point may apply to some business more than others. I know it applies in the life insurance business, but if it does apply, let's be clear on what a call is. If you dial a number and no one answers, that is not a call. It's an effort, yes, but it's not a call. A call is when you call someone and actually gets them on the phone to present your pitch. The question is how many prospects do you need to have on a list so that you can sit there for a while and just make calls to reach and pitch a predetermined amount of prospects. This reminds me of a scene in the movie, "Pursuit of Happiness", with Will Smith, when he was going through the selection process to become a stockbroker. In this scene, he was given a list to call to reach prospect to sell stocks. In the movie he talks about how he fine-tuned that process to make it more effective and him more efficient to sell stocks. Well, in many sales jobs, the same is true. Once you know how many prospects you need to have, you make sure to build and refresh your list so that when you sit to make calls, you can hit your "calls reached" numbers.

Calls to appointments booked – Clearly not every call you reach will give you an appointment. I wish. The question is out of the calls that you reach, how many appointments can you get booked where the prospect agrees to see you and hear your pitch? The more efficient you can be there the better. You may ask what is a good percentage? The real answer is that is not relevant. What is relevant is to determine what your percentage is and seek to improve it every day.

Appointments booked to appointments kept – Never assume that just because a prospect gives you an appointment that it will always keep. Things happen. People forget, issues arise, people intentionally skip your appointment, all kinds of things happen, but over time you get better at determining what percentage of your booked appointments will turn into kept appointments. As you get more mature in your sales career and you deal with repeat clients and people who are referred to you, your kept appointments ratio approaches 100% if not always at 100% because you get very selective with who you meet with, but if you are still growing in your field working that through is important.

Opening appointment to closing appointments – Like I said earlier, in every sales job there are these two categories. You will never get to a closing if there is no opening. You will never get to a sale if all your appointments are openings. Therefore, you always want to maintain a balance between the amount of openings and closing you do in a given period. I have had weeks of all openings. No sales were made in those weeks. I have also had weeks of all closings. Where sales were made, but I had no set up for next week. So, to keep the ball rolling, you need both. Closings to sales. This is your real closing ratio. We will talk about the closing process later, but once you have gone through that process with a qualified prospect, you put yourself in the best position for a sale. The next question is how many sales do you actually close from your closing appointments?

Number of sales – In most if not all sales organizations, administration keeps track of the number of sales. This is often the bases of performance analysis, recognition an rewards. I know that my company kept those records and those records we kept when I sold cars. That's how I still remember the year

1994 when I made salesman of the month I had sold 17 cars. The number of sales completed. You want to know that number. You also need that for bragging rights.

Average size sale – Keep track of the dollar amount of your average sale and if you are in a commission based business, keep track of your average commission per sale. That number tells a story. You should always ask yourself, am I pleased with this market, how can I improve it?

Knowing these activity ratios will be helpful to you understanding how you are doing in your business, where you are weak and where you are strong. The good news is every one of those ratios can be improved with reasonable effort.

In sales, at the end of the year the two numbers that everyone in your company wants to know is how many total units sold and what is the total sales dollar or commissions generated. Your home, spouse, children, or better half only wants to know one number, how much are you bringing home. Put a smile on their faces this year.

CHAPTER 10

The Problem—Solution Nexus

Most of us were taught to think that a problem is a bad thing. Not true. A problem can be the best thing since sliced bread. Think about it. It was a problem that spawned just about every invention and advancement the world has seen. It was a problem that gave us great bridges, planes, ships, computers, TV, electricity and everything else. A problem is why we have our jobs and a problem is why I am writing this book. If everyone in the world who are in sales were doing great, there would be no need. So the first thing really is for us, particularly as salespeople to re-orient our thinking about problems. There is an old Chinese saying that goes, "Do not curse the darkness, light a candle." As salespeople, one of the important value adds that we bring to a relationship is really our point of view, our optimism and can do attitude. As the nature of life and business is, it presents us with new issues and challenges every day. By the nature of things, solving a problem is a part of life. This creates a huge opportunity for us in sales. This is where and how we shine. The thing about situations that people and businesses often find themselves in is that a problem may exists, but sometimes the prospect or client may be aware that it exists and sometimes they are not aware. Ignorance can be bliss, until knowledge, knocks on the door with a spotlight.

One thing I have come to realize is that very often you find that people need a guide. They need someone who knows about a situation to help them navigate to a better place. This reality has little to do with their level of education, fame, income or wealth. None of us knows everything. Then these is the situation where when you, as a trained and knowledgeable salesperson, walks into a place or a situation, you can see where improvements can be had quite readily, but the prospect does not see it yet. This is why when it comes to getting a prospect to the point of looking at a problem together there are two approaches that gets us there. Either there is a need recognition, where the client eventually raises their hand and says, hey, I have this problem. Can you help? Or, more often than not, there is the approach where you as the salesperson who observes a situation and say, hey, I think you have a situation here that can be improved, solved. This is need development. At the end of each of those exercises, you and the prospect will end up at the same place together looking at the problem and saying, ok how can we fix this. If you do not get to that point with a prospect, you do not have a sale in the making. The first step to getting to even the hope of a sale is getting to agreement that a "problem" exist. Now, what for our purpose is a "problem" and how do we fix it. A problem is anything or any situation that does not meet the prospect's satisfaction, and yes, that definition is intended to be as wide as that, but also as specific as that. For us as human beings and businesses, obtaining satisfaction is a temporal and sometimes elusive things. This is good for us as salespeople. We fix problems with solutions that bring satisfaction. In so doing, we make an income. The good thing is that soon enough, for whatever reason, the client will sprout another problem and need satisfaction for it, and the cycle continues. What is key for us to know is that a solution is what brings satisfaction. This is the problem – solution nexus, which brings us to a simple, but very important point in sales. If there is no problem there is no need for a solution. There is satisfaction. What that means is that if you cannot get the client to agree that a problem exists from his or her perspective to the point that they want to do something about it, you do not have a deal. Sometimes salespeople are so enamored with their product that they think everybody should buy one. Great, but if the client does not see your product as a solution to a problem you don't have anything. So where should your focus be? Making clear to all what the problem is, making clear and gaining agreement that life cannot go on with this problem not fixed. Once you have that my friend, you are on the road to a sale.

So the question is, what causes problems? Or, asked another way, why do people buy? What are their buying motives. People buy for one of six reasons, mostly.

1. The desire for financial gain. This one is easy to see. If your product or service will bring them money, you have their interest. If your product or service can help them make more of what they produce, do more or do better where they can realize more money, you have their interest, even if engaging you would cost them more if they can see on balance how they will come out better.

2. The desire to save money or the fear of financial loss – If they are able to produce the same at less cost, that is of interest as well, or if you can show how you can help them mitigate or prevent a loss, that has value as well. Billions of dollars are spent on insurance for this same reason, but there are other products and services whose premise is the same. We can save you money or help you not lose money.

3. Convenience, comfort on ease – How many of us have made a purchase just on these desires alone. Have you not booked a hotel in a city because of its convenient location? Have you not bought a car for its comforts and have you not bought a thing, phone, an app, a device, something because its so easy to use. Especially in this digital, instant world, we are so inclined to these. If what you offer has those features, be sure to highlight them. Even if they are not the main reason for the purchase, they are definitely value added features that can tip the scale in your favor.

4. Protection and Security – You may have noticed how Ring. com just blew up in a short period of time. This just goes

to shoe how interested we are in protection and security. Products and services that offer protection and security comes in different forms, but the point for us here is to recognize that in whatever we are selling if there is a feature that provides a level of protection and security for anything of value to the client, it is wise to bring that to the clients attention. As you know for me protection and security is my bread and butter. That's what we sell in the insurance business, but those qualities exist elsewhere as well.

5. Prestige or pride of ownership – As you know, I sold cars for a while. Let me tell you, I know some people buy cars for the prestige that comes with them. I have sold expensive Cadillacs, Lincolns, Buicks, and trucks. You can almost feel the pride as people drive off in their cars. I remember sometime between 1992 and 1994, the Dodge Viper came out. We had one, just one, in the whole dealership. They were hard to get. This was a new vehicle, by new I mean new make, the first of its kind. We had people from all over biding on that red Viper. That was the first, and I believe last time, I saw a car sold for well over sticker price. Unfortunately, I was not the one to sell it, but just being around that buzz was an experience. I know that prestige and pride of ownership is a buying motive. I've seen that with my own two eyes.

6. Love – Need I say more? Probably not, but I will say a few things. We all know that love is a powerful emotion. People will go the extra mile for love. For us as salespeople, what we need to hone in on is who or what that love emotion is directed towards. There is love of others, family, friends, people, as well as love of self, love of things, love of animals and love of ideas. That reason of love gives us an opening to understand why a client would want to do something. We ought to use that knowledge to help them achieve satisfaction by doing for the object of their love. As an aside, as much as it may not be nice to say, other emotions drive people to buy as well like hate, jealousy and envy. These are not the best

emotions, but they are in fact emotions that drive people to make decisions. I'm not talking about any decision to hurt anyone, but rather decisions to spend money. I want to have a bigger house, bigger car, better phone, nicer clothes than others. Those emotions can drive those desires. Keep that in mind.

When you think about a completed sale transaction you appreciate that there are two sides to that coin. There is the buying side and the selling side. Lets deconstruct those sides for a minute to get a look see into the minds of each side. The buying side goes through a process. We all go through that process but when we are going through it. It is worth looking at the process to understand what is happening at the various steps so that we as salespeople can know where a prospect is in their process and what we may be able to do to impact that process in our favor. I call this Buying process The Buying Mission, like when someone is on a mission to do something. The buying mission is essentially a search for satisfaction. It starts with problem recognition, or put another way, need recognition. Notice it does not start with need development. Why, because need development is not the point at which the client says, I have this problem and I want a solution to it. People get to the need recognition point in a number of ways; your car breaks down on you, you're home watching TV and see an ad for a new phone; your friend buys a new house and now you want one. Problem and need can just as well be a want. The emotional intensity tied to each can be the same. The next step is that the search process starts. People begin to look around for possible solutions. This is when they get in their car and start to drive around on car lots. This is when they start to buy home magazines and drive through neighborhoods. This is when you find them in the Apple store at the I phone counter feeling out options. When salespeople find a prospect in this state, they feel like the person is really to buy. They are not. Further, you pushing them to buy at this point can push them away from you. They are not ready. They are in the information gathering phase. The best thing that you can do during this stage is be understanding and provide them with information. This does not mean not to engage, just give them the brochure and move on. It means engage them at the point where they are which is information gathering. Take the time to ask about the needs, wants, likes, seek to identify their buying motive and clarify any questions they may have. Based on where they are on the continuum, your explanations may close that loop for them. If you are an observant salesperson often times you can tell when they move from I'm gathering information, help me decide to, I have decided now what's the next move. You hope that they do that with you and based on what your product or service is, they will either move to finalize with you right there or come back to you or accept your call when you follow up. However, the information search is the step before evaluation of alternatives step.

This step, evaluating, is the natural next step in the process. If you find someone at the beginning of the information search process, you are not likely to get a sale. They have not seen enough yet. The other day I was in Best Buy looking for a laptop. There were many different ones and I really was confused. I did not know if the differences in price denoted quality, performance, functions that I may never use or what. I really needed an education. Then a salesman come up and explained to me that pricing mainly revolved around speed, storage, features and brand. Once he told me that, even though I was not ready to buy yet, I was able to put the laptops in categories so I knew what I wanted in a laptop and what I didn't. I was able to narrow them down to the few options that had what I needed and interestingly enough, once I narrowed my "have to haves", my options became limited, even in Best Buy with all those laptops there, and my anxiety went away. When I was ready, I called the guy who helped me over and said, this one. So there it is, after the evaluating options process is complete, the natural next step is the purchase decision.

Please do not confuse the purchase decision with the actual purchase. In my example just now, I was actually in the store and I bought at the time. It does not always happen that way. Further based on what kind of business you are in, real estate for example, require a little bit more paperwork to complete a sale. There is an old saying that goes many things can happen on your way to the bank. That is to say that when you think you have everything locked up–the client has said yes, the appointment to sign the papers is set, everything looks like a go—and then out of the clear blue sky, something happens. Some things you cannot control but keep in mind that the purchase is not the purchase until it's the purchase, and some would add, and the check clears your account.

Once the purchase is done, as we are still talking about the buying mission, the buyer does a post mortem, always. Consciously or unconsciously. They evaluate the experience, they evaluate the product or service and they do a value check. Always remember that. How that last part of the buying mission goes has an impact for you. If you are selling insurance, we will discuss delivery later, but be mindful that you are still in the solidifying the sale phase. If you sell almost anything else even if all sales are final, remember all that means is that sale may be final. Don't let your lack of service make that statement true for you for all future sale possibilities. When I sold cars this one day a senior lady came in the dealership. A salesperson served her, not me. She was interested in a Cadillac, a big ticket item. The salesman spent hours working with her. They test drove a number of cars, she was smiling, he was smiling. Finally she came in from the lot. She had decided on the brand new Cadillac she wanted. The process went on for another few hours to negotiate and finalize the sale with all the "T"s crossed and the "I"s dotted. The client drove off as happy as a lark. We all congratulated the salesman on a job well done and a good commission made. In the car business once a brand new car is sold, that's it. It is no longer a new car. The second that car drives off the lot, actually before, once that new owner signs off on it, that's a used car and the value automatically depreciates. All sales are final or so we thought. The very next day here comes the lady back with her brand new, now used, Cadillac, but this time with her son. All I saw was a lot of talking going on between the son and the company higher ups. Next thing I know the impossible happened. A new car that became a used car became once again a new car. The son was quite upset that his mother had bought the car. He came in making the argument that we took advantage of an old lady and he wanted the sale reversed. I had never seen that happen before.

Never even heard of it, but it happened that day. The point? Post – purchase evaluation happens. This time the son got involved. The salesman did not do anything wrong. An old lady does have the right to buy a new car on her own. I was not near to all the talking but the dealership was very quiet that day. I do not know why the dealership did what it did, but I do know that public relations and customer retention are important considerations for any business. I would suppose those two considerations helped in the decision making from the company's perspective.

As a final point on the Buying Mission, keep in mind that customer retention and customer acquisition are two different things but two very important things in their own right. Keeping a customer is always cheaper in the short term and long term than acquiring a new customer. During the Buying Mission do not seek to short circuit the system by trying to push a client to buy who is not ready. This makes both getting and keeping clients more difficult. Take the time to understand the Buying Mission and seek to determine where people are and then help them in that process. They will appreciate you for it.

Then there is the Selling Mission, the other side of the coin. We often use selling and sales interchangeably. The fact is though, they are different. A sale is a simple transaction of value for value. When you go to a fast food restaurant and order your lunch, the restaurant has made a sale, but they really did no selling. They did not take you through the steps to a sale as least not in the usual understanding of selling from a salesperson's perspective. Selling is a process that really follows a step by step rhythm to get to an exchange of value. To be good at sales there are certain things a salesman ought to know and apply. A salesman ought to know that the key to success in selling is focusing on achieving satisfaction for the client. That's the trick. Though that satisfaction may be temporal, it is at that point when the client feels relieved and accomplished. Our goal as salesperson is to get to satisfaction. A very effective method of getting to learn what would satisfy is the Socratic Method which involves asking probing questions about the interest at hand to get a clear understanding of what the client wants. In some businesses the salesperson encounters the client after they have been brought into the company or through some other lead generating method. Sometimes the conversation starts at the need development or need recognition level, not at the prospecting level. If that is your model then it is very important that you take the time to determine where the client is in their buying mission. If you started at the prospecting level, you would know how you connected with the client and whether they had expressed interest or you had to uncover a need or propose a solution to a possible problem they may not realize they had until you mentioned a possible better way. Key point is to not take it for granted that even though the client or prospect was sourced for you that they are really clear and convinced that they need your product. Do the work of identifying the "problem" together.

As mentioned earlier in the book be ready to communicate your value proposition to your client. Regardless of how you get to engage with them, they need to know what you can or will do for them, what your product or service can or will do for them to ad value to their life, their business. Always remember, the reason you exist in business is to deliver value. Make that value unique to you.

When you engage with clients, please do not use techno speak or industry or company jargon. No one knows what that means. Speak English, Spanish or French, Russian or whatever language your client speaks so that you both can be on the same page when you communicate. Sometimes we need to be careful even in the way we say things. I remember my od boss at the care dealership meeting with us, the sales team, one time. He said, guys, be careful what you say to the customers. We would say "Sir, you don't have to worry, we won't miss your business." Well, he said, be careful how you say that. Even though we mean we won't miss your business like an arrow missing a bull's eye, in other words, we will make sure the price is right for you, it could come across like we will not miss your business if you don't buy from us. Lastly, when you are on the Selling Mission, be mindful of the difference between price and cost. In the life insurance business, we always run into the question about whole life insurance versus term insurance. If you don't know, whole life insurance, for the same amount of death benefit, say $100,000.00, costs more than the same amount of death benefit if it were a term policy. This is because Term policies have no residual cash building up in the policy over time, whereas with a whole life policy you will pay more for it, but after a few years it will accrue cash so that later you can recoup your premiums back and then some. So when people would say they prefer term insurance over whole life, we would show them how over time the whole life policy will cost less and have greater benefits. Up front the price of the term policy is less but long term the cost would be more. This concept applies in so many other situations. In real estate a particular house my cost less than another house, but if the up keep over time will require more money, then the cost of that house is really more than the other one. Bringing these points to the buyer for consideration is the responsibility of the salesperson.

The sales process itself has a number of sequential steps. Based on who you ask you may get a different number of steps either, six, seven, ten, for example, but whatever number of steps they give they always follow the same sequential pattern. The process is sequential because that's the way the human mind works. This is why trying to jump the steps is shooting yourself in the foot. The difference in the amount of steps is really the consolidation of a couple of streps at different points of the process. I like the ten (10) steps to a sales because it gives adequate and I believe appropriate attention to all the relevant parts of the process. The ten steps are Prospecting, Pre-Approach, Approach, Fact Finding, Discovery Agreement, Solution Design, Presentation and Close, Sales Follow-Through, Delivery and Service. For the rest of the book we will cover each step. I am aware that every industry has steps to a sale protocol. They may not all line up with these ten steps, but invariably it will incorporate them. So as we go through them, please take what works well for you.

Every so often I come across a good book on the sales process. Recently I read one where the sales process was laid out in four easy steps: Discover, Diagnose, Design and Deliver. As you can see there are similarities between the two. In the business of that book writer either he incorporated the first three steps in the Discover step or in his process the prospects are already existing as clients or there is some other lead generating process that brings new prospects to them. In every business someone, someway, some how has to make contact with new prospects for the first time, even if the prospects come to them looking for a solution to a recognized need. For those you have to find new prospects, the ten steps approach will be quite beneficial.

Everything begins with a problem. Problems are good. They are our friends. Think about it, everyone only gets paid for solving a problem, so do not curse the darkness. Take the problem, find a solution and bring satisfaction to your client. If you do that you will be well paid.

CHAPTER 11

How To Set Up The Ideal Appointment

As I have said earlier, one of the biggest mistakes I see sales people made, regardless of what they are selling, is they talk to the wrong people. Just by correcting that shortcoming in their game alone would increase their closings. Trust me, I know. I have had the misfortunate due to my lack of experience to spend inordinate amounts of time running down, talking to and trying to convince the wrong people to buy insurance. The most grueling work ever. I have come out of appointments, tired and dejected and had to sit back and ask myself how did you get here? And every time, every time the same answer came back to me, you did not qualify. I took the appointment often because I was being lazy, I was desperate, or at a low, but I went out of my market and out of my qualification matrix and ran into a dud.

To be fair, the dud was not the prospect. The bad appointment was not the prospect's fault. It was my fault. Also, please note that the appointment was not a dud because the client was not well off or over aged or not in the right business, the appointment was a dud because I did not qualify the prospect before hand to assess the likelihood of her wanting or needing my product and thereby giving me a good chance at a sale. That's what quality prospecting is about. No, I don't have a crystal ball or a magic wand. What I do have, and what you do have is an understanding of what your product or service does or can do, what value it can bring and with that you can formulate a matrix, a profile of your ideal prospect and seek to talk only to those persons. This is a sales skill.

So lets look at who is a prospect and by default, who is not. What you sell, whatever it is, is designed to solve a certain kind of problem. Whether you are selling to people or companies or countries for that matter, it doesn't really matter. In my business, I sell life and heath insurance. My product is sold to the poor, the middle class and the rich. I have to decide which grouping I want to be my market, and within that market to identify prospects to approach. So the first this I do is crystalize my market, what are the attributes of that group. If its companies you deal with, you want to determine the industry or industries, size, employee count, revenue, profit, budget for your service, location or locations, objectives as disclosed in their annual reports or information generated from other sources, and any other information you need to put them in your definition of your market. If you work with people, you want to consider their age, type of work, maybe the industry, maybe not, for example, if you want to work with accountants, the industry may not be as important. You do want to consider their interests such as sports, politics, hobbies, family, also their lifestyle and style, are they high fliers, bon vivants or low key people, what are their goals and aspirations if you can find that out. How many kids are there, what ages, whether college is in the plans or not. Some of this information will be easy to find, others you will have to ask around or do some digging, but its all good to have.

All of this background information is really just to establish whether someone is in your market or not. Lets say for argument sake, the market you have identified has one thousand companies or ten thousand people in it. What that tells you is for example, if you were going fishing, that is the pool that you would drop your line in. The plan is every time you get a bite, the bite comes from someone in that pool. The fact that that contact comes from that pool is one aspect of identifying a prospect: Is the person in my market, then you can continue down the other qualification criteria. Next, does the prospect have a problem that you have identified. You can make the determination in your business, but in my business clearly not everyone in my market at any given moment has a problem that I can pursue. For example, I have ran into professionals who after a quick conversation, seem to have their insurance matters together. He or she has adequate life insurance and medical insurance. After a quick talk I was able to determine that this person in my market is ok. Move on. On the other hand, I find a professional who just had a baby, is buying a new house, expanding his or her practice etc., yes these are all great signs for me. I have something to talk to them about. So the point is to ask yourself, does this prospect, who is in my market, have a problem that I can help with. That's the second point. Third point. Does this prospect agree that the problem I suspect or have identified actually exists from their point of view. Sometimes you are able to find that out before you get to them, even before you make the call to them. Other times you find that out in the meeting with them. Obviously if you can discover that the problem you think they have can or is being mitigated by something else that they have or have access to then your job of getting a sale my be more challenging. In that case you have to decide if you want to continue to pursue them or not. If you sell cars and you see that one of their cars is old and needs repairs, that may be a good signal, but, if you find out that their parent has several cars and have retired and has offered them access to a replacement car, well, that changes things. For a prospect to be a prospect, you and them have to look at a problem together and say, yes, this is a problem.

The fourth thing you look for is whether the person is willing to consider options to solve the problem. I have gotten caught over the years thinking that because we have identified and agreed on the problem that means that there is agreement to solve the problem. Please, take my advice it does not mean that. Some people and entities are happy to live with a problem for whatever reason. Maybe they have bigger fish to fry and that fish is not in your wheel house, maybe the timing is not right, maybe anything else. Bottom line is they are not open to or ready to address the problem now. Move on.

Fifth, once they are on board with considering solutions, seeing that you are in sales and especially if you work on commissions, the question is can this case go from open to close within your closing cycle. Different industries have different closing cycles. A few years ago, I took the family on vacation to an Orlando Resort. As you might expect, they made my wife and I an offer to attend a timeshare presentation for the resort and other locations. The resort was very nice so we thought why not let's hear them out. I'm from the Bahamas so I'm familiar with timeshare, but I was never the client. This experience did not go well. They pressured and pressured and pressured as again to buy. We did not buy. It was clear that their closing cycle was within that few hours period that they had us there. Their approach was one shot and done. If you did not buy then, they considered you a loss. In real estate, the life and health insurance business the closing cycle can be from one day to one moth. As we've mentioned before, sales is a numbers game, but more so a ratios game. What cases you put in your equation determines your numbers, which determines your commissions, salary, performance chart, all of it. So if the prospect will not close in your closing cycle, you may want to get another prospect, not to drop this one, but add another one to your activity for that period seeing that you cannot count on this one to make the board for this cycle. They may make it for the next cycle.

Another consideration about whether someone in your market is a prospect at the time, number six, is that you know where and how to find them. There are situations where you made contact or got information about a prospect who meets all the above criteria, but you just cannot get to them to complete your process. Oh, I'm so busy I can't meet with you today, but I am interested; next week I'm out of town for a few days, when I get back I have a conference, and after that I take a few days with the family, then I have to study for this new certification, but I wish we can meet, but time is so tight. My friend, you do not have a prospect.

This seventh point is really when you are dealing with a decision making process that involves multiple layers of bureaucracy. You have to deal with operations because that's really where the problem is and the people who are experiencing it, and those who would benefit most from the value that your product or service will bring. However, to get your sale approved, they have to put in a requisition, their superiors have to review, maybe it goes to finance to make a recommendation to management to get a decision. It happens. What do you do in a case like that. Your best bet is to work with the people who are feeling the pain and who would most benefit from the improvement. Help them help you understand the value in terms of savings, more sales, better quality etc. that they will realize with your product or service. Enlist them in your effort to make the call to their superiors and then to finance. Once you enter the zone of finance, you will have to make a financial case, which can be done, but the objective of this point is to point out that to be able to establish this organization as a prospect with promise for a sale, you will need to garner the support of those who will be most positively impacted by the change and value your offer will bring. Do that and you have a live prospect.

Once you have identified and qualified a prospect, what is the next move? Usually a prospect would not be aware that you have them in your sights. So some how or the other you have to make an approach, but before you do, you need to do a little more homework. Get to know the prospect and their situation better. Become them for a moment and think through what their issues and concerns might be and how your offering can solve a problem for them. Gathering information can take place in a number of ways; ask colleagues about the prospect, if the person has employees, that's a good place to get information, if they have a business, patronize the business to get a feel for their organization. All of this is really noninvasive, public domain kind of information sources. The information you want to know is about what the problem is that you suspect he has and how you can help. For example, if you sell computers, a visit to his store may give you insight into systems he may be able to use to operate more efficiently. Technology moves so fast that he may not be aware that your system exists. This approach prepares you for contact with the prospect. People really do respect and appreciate sales people who are aware of what's going on in their industry and if information is available publicly about the company, knowing that is very helpful and understanding what they do and what their issues are is very helpful as well. When you come with some knowledge, you are not a complete outsider. This way your time meeting with them can be more productive in a discussion about the problem. Now to get to that point, you have to make contact. Sales people use all kinds of different ways to make contact and to pave the way before the contact is make. I have used a few different methods. Write an introductory letter that is one page and not too long. Introduce yourself and your company. Share your understanding of the problem they face or the goal they are trying to achieve and briefly share how you can help. The letter says that you will give them a call shortly. That's one way. If you sell something tangible, show and tell is always a good way to get someone's attention. When I sold cars an important step in the sales process is obviously to identify the car that they are interested in. Most of the time we would go on a test drive. That's show and tell, but sometimes the client wants more, so we would let them take the car for the day, bring it back tomorrow. Of course, for us to do that we would have to have a good feeling that doing that would do the trick. Most times it did. Based on what you are selling you can decide the extent of show an tell you can do. Just remember, proof of concept is a very powerful tool. If you can show people that your offering does what you say, you have a very good chance. In my case, seeing that I sold intangibles, I used a phone call to book appointment to make my case. In my call, I would lead with information about what I do and how I can help them. Sometimes I would ask, after I introduce myself and my company, I would ask, Mr. Smith with respect to your medical insurance, if I can offer you a plan that has the same or similar benefits for reasonably less cost, would that be something that interests to you? The point is to lead with a question that you know he or she is likely to have no objections to and of course something you can actually do. Another approach is to lead your call stating what you know their issue is and how you can help and your value proposition to the offer. Mrs. Smith, I understand that you currently use the so & so system in your business. I would like to show you our new very efficient, high speed and high volume system that can save you 20% on operation cost. Further, I give my assurance that in a transition, I will stay with you to make sure everything runs smoothly and that you are realizing the savings.

If your approach is to use the phone, then your call should be broken down into three sections:

1. Who you are and where you are calling from.

2. Why you are calling – state your question or propose or solution.

3. What action do you want them to take – usually its agree to a meeting.

In most cases, a meeting to further clarify, demonstrate or present is needed. Ask for it by suggesting two time options: Is 10:00am on Monday good or is 2pm on Tuesday better. If they are inclined, they will either agree to one or give another option. Keep your call script to 60 seconds. No long deliberation. Do not try to complete a sale over the phone unless you are doing telemarketing and closing sales over the phone is what you do. If your work requires applications to be completed, like mine, documents to review and sign, if your work requires a meeting, do not try to sell over the phone. The purpose of the phone calls is to book the meeting or sales call. Do that and get out. I suggest you take some time to work on your phone script using those three points and keeping it within sixty seconds. Don't rush, don't sound too rehearsed, just flow. Practice with your family, friends and colleagues.

Once you begin to make contact with prospects, invariably you will run into some objections. That is great news. There is a tendency for sales people, especially the inexperience ones to run scared of objections. I understand that. I was there to. I have come to realize that objections are a sales person's best friend. Why? Well, think of it like this. Have you ever been in a conversation with someone and there you are talking and talking and they just sit there, sometimes with a blank face, but more frustratingly with no reaction, no, what did you say? Say that again; you've got to be kidding. These are all feedback to tell you that they are engaged, they are at least listening. Well objections one some what like that. They are guide posts into the mind of the client. When you've been around long enough and you've head many and varied objections you realize that they boil down to four basic types. Once you are prepared for them you can sit comfortably and prepare to address whatever comes. Before I go into the four types of objections, let me share how to handle all objections as a matter of course or routine. My basic strategy is to ignore the objection the first time it is brought up. You would be surprise how many do not resurface after that. People often feel that they have to say something to put you off. When someone raises and objection to me, I would simply agree with them and continue my presentation. "Harold, I hear you, it sounds good, but I can't afford this," My response? I know what you mean, but if you look at this chart over here. "That's the ignore move. Its really not saying your point is not valid or that it is not true, what it is saying is let us give it some more time to see if this really is a problem for you. Like I said earlier, many times that objection does not arise again. But, lets say a new objection arises for the first time, "Man, I'm not sure I have time for this." I use the same approach because it's the first time for that one. The client is grasping for straws. Now, if an objection comes up a second time, I acknowledge it, "I really don't think I can afford this," then I say, Mr. Smith, I understand that affordability may be a challenge, but lets talk about that in a few. Is that okay? Alright then. As I was saying." The fact is sometimes even then the objection does not come up any more and the client agrees to the appointment, gives me a time and off we go. However, in this case I know what's on his mind so I come ready to the appointment with a proposal to address the price issue. Finally, while we are still on the phone trying to book the appointment, he brings up the same objection a third time, I have to stop and address it head on. "Mr. Smith, I do agree that with the matter affordability can be an issue. However, in cases like yours we have a number of payment options and other cost saving measures that we can apply to bring this opportunity in your affordable range to get this problem solved for you." That should calm Mr. Smith down and when we meet, we will discuss in detail the offering, the solution, and the affordability measures.

Now here are the four common objections and how to handle them.

No Money – Mr. Smith, that is exactly why I am calling with our product, we will be able to save you money so that in a short period from now, you would not have to make that statement.

No Time – Mr. Smith, I really understand. Time is tight for me as well. Let's do this, if you give me 15 minutes of your time, I will make it worth your while. If after 15 minutes, I have not piqued your interest, I will leave. Agreed? We can meet over lunch on me.

No Need – Here I often use that old objection response technique, but I always use it honestly and from the heart. I would use feel, felt, found. Mr. Smith, I understand how you feel. If I were in your position and looking at things through your eyes, I would feel the same way too, but after giving your situation some thought, let me tell you what I've found …

No Interest – Mr. Smith, I could understand why you would not be interested, but let me ask, if I can save you 15% on your cost, would that interest you. Or if I can help you increase your revenue or make more sales or operate more efficiently, would you be interested? We just need a few minutes to talk.

Getting that appointment with a qualified prospect from your market gets you half way to a sale, maybe more. The sales skills needed to get to this point comfortably are indispensable. Study this process—like I said, seeing the right people is key.

We've looked at the first two steps to a sale. Prospecting and the pre approach. After identifying the prospect, I consider all the activity up to that point of meeting with the prospect, pre-approach. Some may disagree and include aspects of my pre-approach as the beginning of the approach step. For me, the third step to a sale starts when I'm meeting with the prospect and have to "approach the target" with certain tactics. My approach starts with an introduction and a "Thank you for giving me some of your time," I hope to make it worthwhile for you." When you are in the approach the key things you want to get to are:

1. Pick up from the points you made in the call to get the interview. The points about the problem you understand they have.

2. Seek to get confirmation that "the problem" exists and spend a few minutes sharing your understanding of the problem, what issues it can be causing, how you are familiar with it and how your company has worked hard to deal with situations just like theirs.

3. Share briefly how you would be able to assist. The kind of work you do and the value you can bring.

The goal of this approach section is really to get the prospect comfortable enough with you and your knowledge of the situation so that they move with you into the fact finding, discovery and diagnosing phase. The approach phase is like a preamble to step four. During these first minutes, you really want to build some rapport with the prospect. Remember, people buy from people who they like. To build rapport, I try to find some common ground, something that we can connect on and that she would like to talk about. People like to talk about their family, their hobbies, their career, their sports, things like that and often times you will find something related to them in their office. I would say, tell me about this award over here, where was this picture taken, is that your son? How long have you been at this law firm. These kinds of questions and observations always get a good, positive response and people begin to open up. I let them talk and then at the right time I turn the discussion to why I am here. That is my style. I have read books from other very successful salespeople who prefer another approach. They are more rigid and to the point on business. That may be great for their environment or their personality, but for me, getting to know the person works better. I guess to each his own. The step to a sale leaves room for different personalities, but no room for skipping the step. The next step is fact finding.

CHAPTER 12

Discover The Facts

Continuing on the theme that our job as salespeople is to identify a problem, get agreement from the client that the problem is a problem, and then propose a solution that fits within the clients affordability to bring satisfaction. That's what we do. To do that though, we need information. Up to this now, the whole sales dance is to get us here so that we can become "detectives" and discover or better yet, uncover, facts and feeling about the problem. In different selling settings and industries the fact finding period is different and requires a different kind of skill set. I mentioned earlier that my wife and I had a timeshare encounter that did not go so well. In that industry the time allowed for fact finding is very limited. For those sales persons, the prospecting is often done for them so when they meet the prospect, its their first time engaging so a few things need to happen very quickly, introductions, building rapport, fact finding and close, all within a few hours, max. In other industries much more time is allowed. If you are a real estate salesperson, the client engagement process can go on for days, weeks and maybe even months. During that period you learn more and more about the client and their needs and preferences.

When you start the fact finding process what you want to ask yourself is, why should they buy? It is the answer to that question you are seeking for yourself so that you can use your findings and observations to make the case. The first thing to look for is confirmation of the lack of value. Confirm that the problem either in actuality or in the client's mind actually exists. They do need a new car, they do need a better systems; Yes I can see why they want to move. Whatever you are selling gather information and observations to confirm that you do have a real problem here. As an insurance agent, when I go into a business, I would ask the employees, do you have a medical insurance plan? Have you guys talked about that? Is this something you think the staff would be interested in? Is that something you think management would be open to consider? For me these questions help me to determine if a problem exist an whether this is a good prospect to pursue. If I am dealing with a life insurance prospect, I would have targeted the prospect based on my parameters and my suspicions, but during the fact find I will seek to confirm them. Once you have satisfied yourself that the problem exist, the other move is to determine what the process would be to bring resolution. The process may be as simple as, show me something that work and if I like it, I will buy it, or it can be much more complex.

As we discussed earlier, you want to find out what the motivation is for the purchase, even if it's a situation where you are trying to get them interested in purchasing, the question would be why would they want to. Think through the six buying motives we discussed and try them on for size based on your situation. If its jewelry you sell, then love is the key, but if its machinery, then the key could be saving money or greater efficiency. Try to lock on a motivation and see how hot they are to realize that benefit. If you are working a case where more than one person is involved in the evaluation process, try to build consensus with other teams members. This may require a side conversation to get their feedback and to learn more about the dynamics of the team. Who is the leader either de facto or de jure, who is the influencer, who is considered the "smart one". These are all valuable pieces of information. Spend time learning from the various team members what their point of view is. I have had to deal with situations like this a number of times while working group insurance cases. In those situation, especially when benefits and the actual insurance carrier is changing, there are members on the decision making team who have preferences for certain benefits and those who have "allegiances" to certain insurance carriers. In these cases you really need to focus on the value your offer will bring because sometimes the obvious value compared to the current state is your strongest argument to overcome a push back from some members of the team. Your case must basically say, "Guys, this deal is better for the organization." If it says that, its hard to fight it.

During your fact find, obviously budget is a big thing you want to find out based on your industry, sometimes where the price needs to be may be obvious or at least in a reasonable ball park; but in others, the range is not clear and the room is very tight. In the insurance business, particularly property insurance, you can loose a case for just a few dollars difference in price, literally. However, in the real estate business, usually the prospect gives you a range to work with. On the other hand in the jewelry world the lid is open. Always week to get a feel for what their budget is. To do that, you can ask directly. That will get you an answer to gauge their position or a direct answer. Another way to do it is to give them examples of that option's cost and they would indicate by their response which option they are leaning towards. Getting a fix on their budget is very important because once you are done with your fact find, even if you are dealing with a walk in at a jewelry store, you will have to go work on options to present. If your options are way off, you could loose the prospect right there. People are funny. If you present some prospects with options that are out of their range, rather than telling you that, some people would just stop the engagement, say thank you, and leave. Everybody understands that in a sale, price is a consideration so you trying to find that out up front is not offensive, but later on it could be viewed as you deciding on what you think they can afford.

While you are in the space of talking about the budget if financing is an issue in your business, ask about their funding source. Are they writing a check, getting a loan or raising funding? How will the purchase be paid for? Also, are they looking to pay in installments or one lump sum? Sometimes the terms make the sale. Find out who is/are the key person or persons in the decision making process. I always prefer to deal with the decision maker, but that is not always the case. I often deal with a case where my contact is the HR manager, but the decision maker is the CEO or executive board. Sometimes it is not protocol to reach out to these persons directly. In that case you have to work with your contact to help them make a very good case in your favor.

When you are going through a fact find, certain things start to become clearer. You understand the problem better and your mind starts racing about possible solutions you can present. What I have found is sometimes your standard solutions that are readily available will not work. This is where "think outside the box" really applies. You may have to "create" a solution for the client which may include your standard product along with other products or services within your company, but there are times when you may have to go outside of your company to work with someone else's product or service in conjunction with yours to find a better solution for your client. I know some people will not like to hear that but the fact is that no company has a perfect product for every situation, and if you are committed to looking out for your client's best interest, that really would be the best thing to do. Yes, you may loose some commissions, but your client will appreciate your honesty an professionalism. What ever happens from there, good things will come your way.

Here is a question that I put to clients as I work with them, "In a perfect world, what would the ideal outcome look like for you! This question lets me inside their head to see the world the way they would like it to be. I obviously would try to work towards that ideal, but if they are too far out, I would be irresponsible if I did not bring them back in. Mr. Smith, I will do everything I can, but the likelihood of this coming in that range is slim to none. Or Mr. Smith, given the condition of this property, it will likely take twice that to get it where you want it. People appreciate that because sometimes they just do not know that they are outside the realm of reality. Don't leave them there.

The other thing, do find out what timelines you are working with for execution. Are they ready to go now, next week or they really won't be ready until next year. That's a bummer. That has happened to me. You go through the whole process. Everything is good and looks good, even the budget and the funding. The only thing is at the end, because you did not ask, you find out that they say, "Oh no, we weren't planning on doing this until summer" and its only February.

A good way to find out about their current situation is to ask them what are their likes and dislikes about the current situation. What improvements or changes would be nice to have. At this point you can interject how your solution can make the situation better. Here, too, information about technical improvements found in your product would be handy. Also, your fact find may discover that a visit with your technical team to the client's office may be able to yield valuable intel for your solution. Salespeople should know some features and benefits about their offering, but they are not necessarily the technocrats of their company. Use your tech department when you need to. They can see and explain things that you cannot. As you are all on the same team, when the sale is done, you will get the commission anyway.

Two last points to keep in mind as you do your fact find, current vendor relationships and sacred cows. Keep a look out for ties to the current vendor. Sometimes those relationships are deep and personal with decision makers. Do not say anything negative about the current vendor. You do not know how deep that relationship goes. Focus your discussion around the solution, how it will do this and that for them, how it is good for the organization, its customers and employees. Solidify yourself as a friend of the organization and as a professional. In time you will build relationships with the brass, but now it's the company's interest that you are looking after. Everyone can agree on that. When it comes to sacred cows, don't touch them. You are too new. If they are a real problem, wait some time, maybe even years before you address. Those ties can be very strong. You do not want to be seen as the person who breaks up that relationship or kills the sacred cow. You may not be forgiven, even if you keep the account, someone may be laying in wait for a moment to get rid of you.

DISCOVERY AGREEMENT

The fifth step to a sale is the discovery agreement. This does not have to be a big long thing, but it is a very important check point in the process. The discovery agreement is really just a question, but it's a question asked at a key point in the cycle. Once you have identified the problem, you have determined what the client's motivation is, you know that you are talking to a decision maker, or the person who represents the decision maker, you know the client's preferred outcome, and at this point, there are no other questions, you can ask the discovery agreement question, and it is this, Mrs. Smith, Are there any other issues we need to consider? If I could find a solution that meets your satisfaction and at a price that we can settle on, is it possible that we may have a deal? If she give you positive vibes, you are in a good place, even if she does not say the actual word yes. She might say, well, let me see what you come back with, or its possible especially if she's smiling when she says it, you are in a good place. But, this is also the time when, if you are in trouble on the deal, that may come out as well. The good thing here is you have not presented your solution as yet so you have time to go back into the fact find and look for what you missed or address a lingering concern.

The discovery agreement acts as a pre-cursor to a close. Its intended to let you know where you are at that time. I think it is a great step in any sale engagement with anyone for any product or service. Done as prescribed above, it can save or make many sales. In sales settings where time is way short like in a retail store the discovery agreement can still be used to give direction to the encounter. If after a quick fact find the response to the discovery agreement is positive, then immediately the sales person would look for items that meets the clients criteria. In sales engagements that require longer periods to prepare a presentation, at this point you would book the next appointment date and go prepare the solution to present. Either way, it is a good step to make sure you cover.

CHAPTER 13

Close With Confidence

I have sold many things in my life, newspapers, sea shells, straw dolls and bags, as well as different kinds of insurance. In every case, no matter how long the interaction, there is a point, sometimes just a moment, when I had to think about solution design. When I sold conch shells, thats a common form of sea shell in the Bahamas. Tourist would stop by our shop looking for a souvenir. After a brief fact find, I would get an idea of what they were looking for, then I had to select options to show them. Sure this is not a new idea, or revealing point, but that is my point. Every sales endeavor, even the simplest ones, have an element of solution design. As the sales engagement get bigger and more complicated, solution design becomes more and more important for several reasons: 1. To make sure that the technical aspects of the sale are covered including contract points, features and benefits, etc. 2. The extra, value added aspects of the offering to differentiate the product or experience from the competitor. So the key focus when designing a solution to present is on delivering the value that you've been talking about. Remember, the value is not only the product, service, advice, delivery, support that will bring satisfaction to the clients experience with you. Think about the client's hot button. What is their motivation for this? Think about their budget both now and later. If you sell someone a computer system for example, and they cannot afford to maintain it, even if they were able to make the initial investment for it, that's no good for them or you. Be sure to consider appealing to the heart and head. Emotions often drive a sale, but when the client gets a chance to sit back, they consider whether the purchase was wise financially. Deal with that in your solution design. For example, the $40,000.00 car has all the bells and whistles you like, a little more room and the leather interior, but it's a stretch. Show also the $30,000.00 model, with a few less options, but still a great buy, but definitely much easier on the pocket. You must cater to heart and head and let them decide. That way in the morning after the emotions step back, they will not have it out for you because you "pushed" them in a certain direction. Based on your line of businesses, to bring the solution they need may require multiple product and/or other interventions to make things work smoothly together, but getting all of them on time would be too costly or the client may need more of your product to really do what they need, but they cannot afford all now. You engaged the client to bring a solution that would satisfy. The best thing to do is to plan to explain the entire package that's required to do the job fully. Also, be prepared to offer a game plan over time to get them what they need. Sometimes you can start now and build as you go, other times you may have to recommend that you delay the purchase until the client can do the right thing. People appreciate that honesty. One last thing on solution design. If you are selling something like insurance that they can go elsewhere and get, seek to add something of value that's the others are not offering. This can be a service offer, if it's a car, warranties, a unique configuration, a free home design session, or any other added value benefit. The solution design step is one point in the sales process where you may want to share your thoughts with your boss or trusted colleague to get feedback and ideas before you present to the client.

PRESENTATION AND CLOSE

Step seven is the ask for the money step. The presentation and close. When salespeople get to this point, they get jittery. I understand why, but that does not have to be so. I have learned to control my jitters by doing a few things. 1. Remind myself that the world will not come to an end if this deal does not go through. I can find another one. 2. I have done a proper fact find, I know what this client needs/wants. 3. I have prepared as good a solution as can be prepared by anyone. 4. I have done all I can to get the client to like me, or at the very least not engender a put off attitude towards me. I am ready to make this presentation. That's the most you can do. Now here are a few points for before the actual presentation. Seek to present to the decision maker, if you can. If not, speak to their direct representative. Identify possible causes for a delay in their purchase decision ahead of time and if you can, make adjustments to mitigate them so that your presentation can flow straight into a decision. If the boss is out of town for a week and they will not get to discuss your proposal with him until he gets back, try to move the presentation date to when he is back in office. Your goal is to have things lined up so that within 48 hours after your presentation, you can get a decision. That would be ideal. Things only stay hot for so long. Review your presentation to make sure you clearly identify the problem and the solution your offer will bring. Test it out on someone. The answer you are looking for from them is that this proposal makes sense. If I were them, I would go with it.

Here is a mistake that I've seen salespeople make. So I want to share with you so you don't. They go to a presentation, the clients say yes and are ready to go, but the salesperson left the paperwork to take the order at the office. Don't do that. Make sure you have everything you need so that when the client says yes, you are ready to solidify that sales. Remember back when we talked about the buying mission, a purchase decision is not a purchase. A purchase is not a purchase until it's a purchase. When you leave that moment when they are hot and go to get stuff, by the time you get back all kind of things could have happened. The client gets a call from someone selling something else, an emergency arises that puts the purchase off, this happens or that happens. But, if you have everything right there, when you leave they would have bought and whatever happens after, they know they have already committed to your sale. So, make sure all your ducks are in a row. As you prepare to make the presentation, if this is one where you are presenting to a board or executive team and the people who will benefit from your solution are not on that board, if possible, get a statement or two from them expressing their support and backing up your claim of value. They know that because you spent time with them in the fact find and maybe even did a demonstration. They are convinced your solution will work. If possible, get them to come in on the presentation with you and speak in person. If you are allowed or able to, speak to a few of the board members ahead of time to get them on your side. All of this can help.

PRESENTATION

At the actual presentation the first step is to review the problem. Do not assume that everyone knows what it is and what the adverse effects or lack of value it is causing. Are they losing money, can they be making more money, is it really outdated and inefficient and causing customer dissatisfaction? These are point to show in your first slide. If this is a personal selling situation, you want to do the same thing, maybe not with a power point, but the key is to establish what the problem is and its negative impacts. I have engaged with a few real estate agents before. What I find with them is that they engage with me only on the property we are looking at or looking for. They do not reference or inquire enough about the situation I am in now and what about it that has me looking for another place. If they did that, they can speak more definitively to how their offers can solve my current needs. Also, especially, if you are dealing with a group of people like a board, you will find that there are people in a decision making role who do not know or do not appreciate the extent to which the problem is a problem. Don't assume that they know. Spell out the problem and its impact. Start off like this, "I have had the opportunity to investigate this issue and its impact on your operations. This is what I found." They will want to hear that, especially from an outsider. If you have someone from the inside to speak to your point, this would be a good place to slot them in, but only to talk about the impact the problem is having.

Once you have everyone on that page its timed to bring the solution. Describe how your solution will solve each of the points of impact you indicated. Each one. Do not put up a point of impact that you do not have a solution for. This is where you go into detail to explain the solution. There will be questions, you want that. The more questions the better this means that they are wrapping their heads around your proposal. The questions also give you a feel for the direction of their thinking. Do not rush this period, do not use techno language that they may not understand. Allow time for what you say to sink in. Remember, you already thought it all through. For them this is their first time hearing it. By now you should know what their buying motives are or should be. Hit on that. Is it saving, efficiently, better customer service etc.?

I realize that I have been referencing a corporate presentation scenario, but let me say that this approach applies to one on one as well. The great thing is you are dealing with the decision maker. Note that as part of laying out the solution, this would be a good time to bring back the in house guy to speak about experiencing, through your demo, that your product works.

The third part of your presentation deals with the finances. Cover both the price and the cost. If you are fortunate, your price would be low or reasonable and your cost, which includes any additional, especially unexpected, out lays of funds they may encounter, even that would be low. But if your price is high, you need to show how it is a good value and if your cost is high, you need to show how the value outweighs that. Will the higher cost yield more sales and therefore a higher aggregate margin? The impression often is that lower price is the better deal. Price can tell a lot of things, but in itself, it cannot speak to satisfaction. The determinant is the price to value proposition. If the price is higher, but I can clearly see better value, I will buy it if I can afford it. There are many people out there who accepts that position. My point here is not to sell on the bases of price. Sell value, sell satisfaction. The fact of the matter is there are many low price, low quality products out there and they sell. More importantly, their buyers are satisfied with them. Not everyone is in the high price, high quality market. Know your market and seek to obtain satisfaction for your client. One more point here, before you make your presentation to the client, run it by your boss or a trusted colleague. Again, if they say, this makes sense to me, you probably have a good case.

After you hit those three points in your presentation—the problem, the solution and the money you are ready to go for the close.

CLOSING

If you have followed the process above, closing should not be a problem. By the time you get here, everyone is clear on why they should buy your product, what it would cost and the value it will bring. To you, your proposal makes sense for the client. You would have covered money questions by this point but just to clear the air, I would ask, are there any more question? If no, then if you are dealing with a personal purchase like a car, insurance or real estate, I would say great, this solutions appears to work for you, I would like to proceed. How would you like to pay for this? Cash, check or credit card? Another closing approach I would use at this point, I pull out the forms and say this is the application form. Is Mark your first name? If this is a corporate sale in that board room, I would say, ladies and gents, this solution seems to work well for you and makes sense to me. I would like to proceed with getting this in place for you. To do that I just need your signature on the purchase order and we can proceed. Do not be afraid of going for the close. You have done the work and you have found a solution. Remember, they have a problem. Closings are difficult when sales persons do not go through the process we just laid out. If you go through the steps, beginning with step one, you put yourself in a very good position to close the sale, but you have to go through the steps. I find that salespeople who spend little time doing what we just discussed, right market, right prospect, right fact find and right solution, spend an inordinate amount of time in their client engagement trying to close compared to the time in the pre–close. Their modus operandi looks like a triangle with the broad side at the bottom.

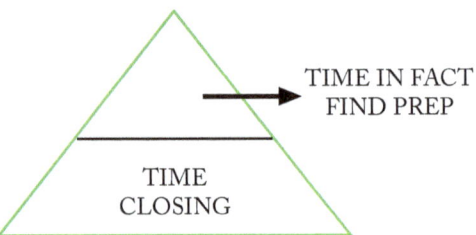

The approach I have been sharing with you actually turns the triangle upside down and allocates most of the time in the pre-close period to preparation and fact finding, discovering, diagnosing and preparing or finding a solution, which then requires much less time in the closing.

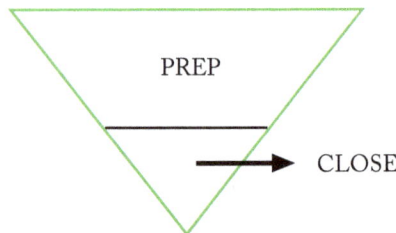

In this approach, by the time you get to asking for the sale, you have made a credible case, all questions have been answered and asking for the sale to effect the value you discussed is part of the course. You actually look like you are doing them a solid. Think about it. When you go in to see a doctor, you have a problem. Then he does the does the work by identifying what the problem is, agreeing with you that it is a problem, then prescribing a solution. You walk out of his office feeling like he did you a solid. You don't feel taken. That's exactly how your clients will feel. Further, when the doctor given you his bill, he does not feel guilty, nor do you by the way, because you got a solution to the problem. As salespeople, we are doctors in our own way. Own it.

FOLLOW THROUGH

The eighth step to a sale is follow-through. In other representations of steps to a sale, this step may be included in another step. I like the idea of pulling it out because it is in itself a valuable point. Sales do not close themselves. Once the client agrees to go with the purchase, follow through means to move quickly to complete the sales contracting process. In some businesses, completing a sale is very simple and straight forward. You issue an invoice and the client pays. That's done, but even in that case, you have to issue the invoice. Do not rest on that sale until the invoice is issued and paid. Yes, I know it sounds simple, but believe me, sales have been lost because paperwork was not completed timely. As a rule, I operated on the basis that people are hot for about 48 hours. Work on getting the deal signed, sealed and delivered in that time frame if you can. Clearly in other industries like insurance and real estate the full sale completion process is a two if not three step dance. In insurance the application comes first then there is the underwriting process before the case is finalized. In real estate its similar, contract, legal and finalize. In the car business you can go from introduction to driving off the lot in a couple hours. Whatever your process is in your business, the point is when you get that green light, don't sit on it. Get the client under signature asap. Getting them committed on paper makes them feel like they have bought. That is what you want.

Another thing, during the follow through process, make it as smooth and painless as possible for the clients. If there are forms to be signed which you can take to them, do that. If they need a ride to get a document, take them. Whatever you can do to make the process smooth and painless, all of that will help with this sale and set you up for referrals and other sales.

DELIVERY

Delivery is the ninth step to a sale in our ten step process. Delivery has several components to it. First and foremost, delivery does not only mean taking the product to the client. Delivery means delivering on your value proposition and confirming that the client is satisfied. If your value proposition includes an element of making sure the client is pleased after the purchase, you should call them.

If you sell furniture, cars, computers, real estate, yes, insurance, and just about any tangible thing, appliances etc. You should make sure that things went will with the delivery, things fit, they are pleased, ok, we're all good. Another aspect of the delivery step is to make sure all the paper work and contractual matters are complete. If things go for too long, people forget and in becomes a problem later. Based on the kind of business you are in, you may want to set up a follow up call to make sure things are still going well. Once all of the above checks out, then it's time to ask for referrals. Hey Mr. Smith, you seemed to have had a great experience. You seem pleased with your purchase. I am very happy that I had a hand in that. I would like to offer my service to other friends and family you have. Do you have a family member, friend or colleague who may be able to benefit from my service? When I call them, is it ok for me to use you as a reference. Thank you so much.

SERVICE AFTER THE SALE

The tenth and final step to a sale is service after the sale. If you are in sales you want to always be available to assist your clients after they have bought anything from you. In some industries, service after the sale is more important, expected or required than others. In discovery above, I talk about setting up a follow up call. That is service after the sale. Remember, for the client, this experience started with you offering to help them solve a problem by delivering a certain value. This is the time to check up on the client after the delivery to make sure that they are actually experiencing the savings, new sales, better customer service, efficiency that you promised. If they are not and you know they should be, this gives you the opportunity to fix things before the client begins to call you names. Sometimes the value is not being realized because the item was installed wrong, they are not using the best parts with it, the employees are not trained on the product or any other of a number of things. That service follow up is key. The client has to realize the value. The service time, even if things are going well, may offer an opportunity to show how things can go better or now that they believe, they may want to get more. Some sales people operate on the one and done premise. Once the sale is done, I'm gone and you're on your own. That is a recipe for failure. During the service after the sale, the tension about the sales process is gone and you and the client can connect as friends. This allows a relationship of trust to build and once that happens, you have a client for life.

CHAPTER 14

Product Knowledge

Knowing your product is as important to a salesperson as each of the other four secrets to success in sales. You cannot be a good salesperson without it. Why? Because the product or service is the source through which the solution comes. The solution is not just the physical product or service that brings satisfaction. The solution entails the feelings, peace of mind, pride, hope, security, and many of the emotions that acquiring a particular product or service can bring. For those person's in the fashion world, they know how just changing a person's clothes can change their attitude, raise their confidence and bring out a whole new person. Sales people in the car business can testify how buying a new car lifts people spirits and even self-image. A new homes give a feeling of hope and security, and so forth. Products are not just physical things, they are emotive things as well. A successful sales person knows that and uses that to her and her client's advantage. There are salespeople, successful ones at that who sell on what a product can do for you more than what the product can do or is. I am not so sure that everybody buying a $200,000 Ferrari is as concerned about what the car can do as they are about what being seen in the car can do for them. I would be interested to know, if this is even knowable, how many $200,000 Ferrari owners ever took the car out to see what it can really do. The point I'm making is that a salesperson really needs to know not only the technical aspects about their product but the intangibles as well. This is true about cars and clothes, but its also true about dishwashers, other home appliances, laptops, phones and the list goes on. Each of them evoke a certain level of pride, feeling of advancement being with the in crowd, you know, just getting ahead in life. Years ago, when my wife and I needed to get a new refrigerator we went down to the store and started looking around. Growing up in my mother's house we always had a plain vanilla refrigerator. Nothing special, no bells or whistles. When I got married and all through college the only places we could afford had the same old style refrigerator. Finally this time, I am now out of college, I am experiencing some success in sales, I think I want to just go for it. So we bought one of the new style refrigerators with the ice and water dispenser on the outside. You should have seen me when that thing was installed. I was so proud of myself, that I could do that. I felt like I had moved up in life. That's what a refrigerator did. At a sales conference, I remember this story about a couple who went to buy a yacht. The first salesman they went to told them all about the yacht, its speed, engine size, width, length, capacity and so on. He knew his stuff, but the couple did not buy. They went down to another yacht and the salesman took another approach. He talked about how they can enjoy sailing through the islands together, having lunch on the deck, sun bathing in their swim suits and so on. He got the sale. Keep in mind that people buy a product or an outcome not for the product. Products that offer comfort and convenience should be sold on that basis, comfort and convenience. The features and benefits are there to facilitate comfort and convenience. When you speak to those features, remember that the technical aspects are there to make good on that comfort and convenience selling point.

When I sold trucks I had to learn the technical aspects of trucks. One reason for that is because in Oklahoma, those people know their trucks. I had to know the various engines, the towing capabilities, about slip differential, four wheel drive and torque. That's truck language. For these buyers, a new truck gave them a warm and fuzzy feeling as well, they loved a new truck, but you couldn't sell it to them if you did not know your stuff. The interesting thing is that at the same dealership, I sold Cadillacs as well. When showing those cars, I focused on the luxury and the new features and gadgets, the seat heaters, the six disc CD player, the automatic a/c system. On the test drive we would talk about the smooth ride, the pick up the engine had, the sound system and the feeling you get when your friends see you in it. Totally different engagement. We would spend less than 30 seconds looking at the engine. Every product was created and designed to solve a particular problem. You may be in the business of selling farm equipment, heavy duty equipment, high tech computers or passenger jets. In every such case, learn what your product capabilities are. When I sold trucks, at first I could not understand the need for a four wheel drive until a co-worker explained to me what those things can do in the snow, in the woods and in wet terrain. Now I know and respect four wheel drives.

In the real estate business they have a term often used in valuing a property. The term is, "best and highest use" of the property. We need to apply this concept to everything we sell. The goal is to get the client to experience the best and highest use of the product or service. That is what it was designed for. When a client underuses a product, they are not getting its value. One reason for that can be that we did not educate the client about the best and highest use of the product and its capabilities. Another reason is that the product may need other things to go with it so that it can perform at its best. Those other things may be at additional cost and they may even have to be sourced from some where other than you. It is important that you help the client maximize to use of the product you sold him. My wife recently bought a new phone. Not too long afterwards she starred having issues down loading messages sent from family and friends. When we investigated, we discovered that the type of phone she was sold had a very limited memory, but the salesperson did not advise her what would happen in that case and recommend that she purchase a memory card. Now we are not in our twenties so she is not at all on those social media sites every day, but in this day and age, just about anything you do on a phone requires a certain amount of memory. Now the client, my wife, is frustrated with the phone and want to get rid of it. That's what happens. So, if your product can be enhanced with other value added features, share that with your client. Let them decide whether to get it or not. They will feel like you are looking out for them.

When you sell a product that requires service, like cars obviously, but other products as well, make it clear to the client what the service requirements are. I would even go a step further. Diarize in your note book a date for you to call and remind them about the service. It would not take a lot of time, but that kind of consideration will go a long way. Last thing on this point. Manage the delivery time line for the client. When you sell something that needs to be delivered, lets say furniture, you are excited when the sale occurs. The client is excited when the furniture arrives to their house. Two things, number one, if you can, manage the delivery process to make sure that the correct item is delivered. A few years ago, I bought a new sofa that was to be delivered just before Christmas. The family Christmas event was happening at my house so I wanted everything to be in place. The delivery truck came the last night before Christmas day and brought the wrong thing. Steam came out of my nose, ears and mouth. Second thing, if you can, manage the delivery so that it is delivered on time. I say if you can because I know in some large operations the salesman has no control over that, but what you can do is manage the client's expectations and leave your number with them so they can contact you if something is not right. Confirm when the product is delivered and call them to make sure all is well.

Knowing the intangible values and the technical aspects about your product go hand in hand. The fact is that every product that is sold has a measure of both of those attributes, some obviously more than others. As a salesman, you really need to know both, you need to know when to apply each one based on your client and your field. The buying experience the client remembers has a lot to do with how you make them feel about the product, about themselves and about you.

CHAPTER 15

Wrap Up

Let me share with you why I decided to write this book. A few years ago, a former agent of mine was hosting a seminar for small business owners and asked me to do a session on how to improve your sales. I prepared my power point presentation and was ready to share. My session started at 11am and was set to run for an hour. At 12pm I had not gotten through the first few points of my presentation. The next speaker was there for her 12pm session, but the attendees were there anxious for me to continue to share. They were like sponges and they wanted more, and I had so much more to share. That session made me realize that there was not an open source for training in my area that I knew about. I'm sure companies did internal sales training, I know we did, but for the general public and small business owners there was no course, no sessions, no place to go that was local. So I said I will offer sales training seminars open to the public. I held a few session, which went well, but I wanted to reach a wider audience and, in this digital age, I wanted to create a resource that people can access anytime, anywhere so I created my "Become a Sales Warrior" course which can be found on Udemy. The course revolves around the five secrets to success in sales. The course maintains a very high rating on Udemy. Shortly after creating that course, a friend suggested that I make a book out of the course and here we are.

I sincerely believe that if you are in any kind of sales work and you apply the five secrets I shared in this book you can substantially increase your sales, increase your income and change your life. If you followed my recommendations herein; you would have written down your dreams, set goals as well as create a game plan to achieve those goals. You would have put on your mental armor to ready yourself for this journey and devised your strategy. You would have covered the skills needed to be successful in this career and you would have realized product knowledge requirements to serve your clients with excellence. You are ready to face the world. I wish you all the best. Good luck.